Till Death Do Us Part

ISBN: 978-0-578-06495-6

All Scripture quotations are from the King James Bible 1611.

Visit our website at:
www.oldpathsjournal.com
www.domelleministries.com

For more copies write to:
Allen Domelle Ministries
PO Box 19
Inwood, WV 25428
or call (304)839-9531

$\mathcal{D}$edication

When I first came up with the idea of writing a book on marriage, my first thought was to use this occasion to honor a special couple who took the phrase, "Till death do us part..." seriously. That couple is my grandparents, Pete and Florence Domelle.

At the writing of this book, they have been married for 71 years. They came from a generation that took their marriage vows seriously. My grandfather has personally told me that everything was not always easy, but he said that they made a promise to each other, and they have kept that promise. Now they are a couple who in their senior years are enjoying the benefits of fulfilling their marriage vows.

Their marriage has withstood the Great Depression, five wars and thirteen presidents. Though tough times have come and gone, they honored their vow, "Till death do us part." I am honored to call them my grandparents and feel privileged to have known such great people. I dedicate this book to them, for I personally know of no one who is more deserving of having a book on marriage dedicated to them than my grandparents.

Table of Contents

Foreword

I am very pleased to be able to recommend to you this book on the subject of marriage. I have known Allen Domelle and his wife, Sandy, for many years. They have a successful marriage, and they understand what the Bible teaches about this important matter.

Bro. Domelle travels across the country strengthening marriages in his preaching and teaching, and he has put into the pages of this book those truths and principles. This book is very practical, scriptural, down to earth and will help any marriage.

One of the great needs of this generation is teaching on this important relationship: marriage. I just know that you will enjoy reading the pages of this book as much as I have. Only Heaven will tell the great work that this book will accomplish in the marriages of God's people.

Dr. Jeff Owens
Pastor
Shenandoah Bible Baptist Church
Martinsburg, West Virginia

"For a marriage to be successful, we must learn what God's purpose is for instituting marriage."

Chapter 1

God's Purpose for Marriage

Before any endeavor is started, a purpose for that endeavor must be established in order to have success. An endeavor without a purpose is sure to fail. An endeavor without a purpose is like shooting guns without a target. Can you imagine going to practice your accuracy with guns and not having a target? There is no enjoyment in that. An endeavor without a purpose is also like combining a bunch of ingredients hoping that something good will come out of that mess. Though you may hope something good can come out of those ingredients, without a purpose for putting those ingredients together, the flavor those ingredients produce could be very distasteful.

Likewise, a marriage without a purpose will head in a direction that leads nowhere. A marriage without a purpose will not be as enjoyable as it should be. A marriage without a purpose will produce a product that could be very distasteful for both parties involved. In order for your marriage to succeed, you must have a purpose.

The attack against the marriage is not a new thing. Immediately after God instituted marriage, Satan began his attack against it so that it would fail. Satan hates the institution of marriage because of what it represents. Therefore, it should not surprise us when we experience attacks against our marriages.

Marriage is a representation of the relationship that the church should have with God. The Scriptures teach us that the church will be the future bride of Christ. Ephesians 5:25-27 says, *"Husbands, love your wives, even as Christ also loved the church, and gave himself for it; That he might sanctify and cleanse it with the washing of water by the word, That he might present it to himself a glorious church, not having spot, or wrinkle, or any such thing; but that it should be holy and without blemish."* As you can see from these verses, the church will be the bride that is to be presented to Christ at the Marriage Supper of the Lamb. Therefore, it is important that our marriages fulfill their purpose because they picture the future bride of Jesus Christ.

According to Webster's 1828 Dictionary, the word "marriage" is defined as, "The act of uniting a man and woman for life." It is amazing that way back in the 1800's they clearly understood the Scriptural definition of marriage. You would think that this definition would not be hard to understand, but with Satan's attack against marriage, the very meaning of marriage is being challenged in our modern day world.

For a marriage to be successful, we must learn what God's purpose is for instituting marriage. If your marriage is going to be happy, fulfilling, and successful then you must fulfill the purpose that God has for marriage.

Proverbs 29:18 says, *"Where there is no vision, the people perish: but he that keepeth the law, happy is he."* You will never have a vision for your marriage without a purpose. According to the Scriptures, without a vision a marriage will die. When I say die, I am not just talking about the couple getting divorced, I am talking about the joy and life of a marriage being gone. A marriage that has no vision will lose its life and cause a couple to simply endure their time together. It is very important for you to understand the purpose of marriage so that you can have a vision for your marriage.

Having a right purpose for your marriage is very important. Just like there are right and wrong purposes for everything else in life, there are also right and wrong purposes for marriage. A wrong purpose for marriage will lead you to have bad and potentially devastating results. Your goal should be to have the right purpose for your marriage so that it will be as happy as God intended it to be.

In order to understand the purpose of marriage, we must go to the Scriptures to find out why God instituted marriage. The Scriptures say in Genesis 2:23-25, *"And Adam said, This is now bone of my bones, and flesh of my flesh: she shall be called Woman, because she was taken out of Man. Therefore shall a man leave his father and his mother, and shall cleave unto his wife: and they shall be one flesh. And they were both naked, the man and his wife, and were not ashamed."* In these verses, we can see several purposes of marriage. Let me give the background of these verses before we go into God's purpose for marriage.

God spent most of creation preparing this world for the being that He would create for Himself. Everything that God created in the world He created for man's enjoyment. You will notice in all of creation, God spoke everything into existence with His word, but when it came to man God used His hands to create him. I believe this is because man was special to God. On the sixth day, God formed man out of the dust of the ground and breathed into his nostrils the breath of life, and the Scriptures teach us that man became a living soul.

After man was created, God gave man the responsibility of caring for His creation, but God saw that man was lonely. God made man for Himself and God was pleased, but God had not made someone for man that would help make man complete. Because of this, God put Adam to sleep and performed the first surgery this world ever had. God took a rib out of Adam and made a woman from that rib. When Adam woke up from surgery, he saw what God made for him and he called her a woman. This act of God is when

9

the first marriage was instituted. You can see in the verses above that man and woman became *"one flesh."* As we look at this first marriage, we can learn the purpose of marriage. In the next several pages, I will point out God's purpose for your marriage.

1. Marriage is between a man and a woman.

Genesis 2:22 says, *"And the rib, which the LORD God had taken from man, made he a woman, and brought her unto the man."* Notice in this verse that God brought a woman to the man. God did not bring a man to a man or a woman to a woman. God intended for marriage to be between a man and a woman.

It is a sad thing in our day that we are battling the very definition of what a marriage is. The sodomite movement of our day is trying to make two people of any sex living together a marriage. God **NEVER** intended for marriage to include sodomites. Though this may not be a popular statement to some, we cannot ignore the fact that God is the One Who established this precedent.

How foolish it is for people to try and go against the very One Who established the very purpose and foundation of marriage. When Henry Ford made the first car, he didn't make the first car to fly in the air or to float down some river. He made the first car to drive down the street. Can you imagine the car telling Henry Ford that it wants to fly and its not going to drive down the street? As ridiculous as this may sound, this is how ridiculous it is for us to try and change the very definition of marriage. We have no right to say that marriage can be between the same sex, for we are not the ones who instituted marriage, God is. Therefore, only God has the right to say what a real marriage is, and He said that marriage is to be between a man and a woman.

2. Marriage is to be established before God.

Again, look at Genesis 2:22 when it says, *"And the rib, which the LORD God had taken from man, made he a woman, and brought her unto the man."* Notice the first marriage was established before God.

From the very start, I believe it is very important to involve God in your marriage. The best way to do that is to have your marriage performed in a church. Though I have no personal quarrels against any justice of the peace, they are not God's representatives; they are representatives of the courts.

I believe the Scriptures make it clear that marriage is a vow that a man and a woman make to each other before God. Therefore, I think it is very important that a man and a woman get married by a representative of God; your pastor. I know there are some who read this who were married by a justice of the peace. I am not saying that you're not married, I just believe it is better to perform your vows before one of God's representatives. If you are one who was married by a justice of the peace, you might want to consider reconfirming those vows privately in your pastor's office.

3. Man was created for God.

God said in Genesis 1:26, *"And God said, Let us make man in our image, after our likeness..."* Of all the things that God created, only man was created after the likeness of God. The purpose of man's creation was to serve God.

When a man understands his purpose of existence and lives to fulfill that purpose, then man will be happy. One of the problems marriages have today is that the man has lost the purpose of why God created him. God purposely created the man first because he was to be the head of the home. It is interesting the man was not made for the woman, but man was made for God. When a man realizes that he was made

11

to serve God and fulfills that purpose, then he will be a better husband to his wife. Any man who runs from the purpose of serving God will not be the husband he should be. A man will only be the right kind of husband if he serves God.

4. Woman was made for man.

Genesis 2:18 says, *"And the LORD God said, It is not good that the man should be alone; I will make him an help meet for him."* Now notice that the whole reason why the woman was created was to be a help to her husband. A woman will not be the wife she should be until she realizes that her purpose in marriage is to help her husband.

Ladies, you will never please God with your life until you fulfill the purpose for which you were made, and that is to help your husband. Notice that woman was made to be a *"help meet"* for man. The words *"help meet"* are two words and not one. Though we will deal with this subject later on in this book, in order to fulfill your role in marriage, you must live to help meet your husband's needs.

5. Marriage was intended to be one couple.

I fear that this is so basic that many people will stop reading, but I beg you to continue reading. Sometimes the very basic things are what we tend to miss when we study the Scriptures.

Genesis 2:24 says, *"Therefore shall a man leave his father and his mother, and shall cleave unto his wife: and they shall be one flesh."* Notice that God said the man and woman were to be *"...one flesh."* God never intended for more than one man and woman to be involved in the marriage relationship.

This is why extramarital affairs are wrong. God only intended for a man and a woman to enjoy each other in marriage. This is also why polygamy is against the Scriptures.

If God intended for there to be more than one man and woman in the marriage relationship, then God would have established this at the very beginning. Instead, God established the marriage relationship to be between a man and a woman. If you are going to fulfill the purpose God intended for your marriage, then you must keep yourself for your spouse alone.

6. The woman is to follow the man.

Genesis 3:16 says, *"Unto the woman he said, I will greatly multiply thy sorrow and thy conception; in sorrow thou shalt bring forth children; and thy desire shall be to thy husband, and he shall rule over thee."* This verse comes after Adam and Eve had committed the first sin. As God approached Eve to punish her, He told her that her desire would be to her husband. In other words, she was to follow her husband's leadership.

What got this first marriage in trouble was Eve taking the leadership role in the marriage instead of following her husband's leadership. Satan attacked this marriage by getting Adam and Eve to switch the roles that God intended for them. Adam followed Eve instead of Eve following Adam, and the result was sin entered into the world.

If your marriage is going to be what God intended for it to be, not only must the woman understand that she was made to help meet her husband's needs, but she is to follow him as he leads.

7. Man is to be the breadwinner of the home.

After God spoke to Eve and told her she was to follow her husband, He then told Adam in Genesis 3:19, *"In the sweat of thy face shalt thou eat bread, till thou return unto the ground..."* God was establishing the roles of marriage to Adam and Eve so they would avoid having any further

13

problems in their marriage. God told Adam that his role and purpose in the marriage was to be the breadwinner.

Men, it is your responsibility to make sure that the bills are paid and that food is on the table. In today's society, the roles have switched where man is the mom and the wife is out making the living. This is wrong! God commanded the man to be the one who makes the living for the home. Men, your wife will never have the security she needs until you become the breadwinner of the home. You need to do whatever you can to be the breadwinner so that your wife does not have to work outside the home. This is one of your roles in marriage.

8. Marriages are to produce children.

One of the best arguments against sodomy is this point. God commanded the husband and wife to have children in Genesis 1:28 when He says, *"And God blessed them, and God said unto them, Be fruitful, and multiply, and replenish the earth..."* God commanded Adam and Eve in this verse to multiply, or have children.

I want you to notice that children are to be born inside of marriage and not outside of marriage. There are many people today who have children before they get married and this is wrong. Children are to come after a couple gets married.

To those couples who don't want to be bothered by children, you must understand that when you took the vows of marriage, you also took the responsibility to have children. To be selfish and live for yourselves is disobedience to God. If it is physically possible, every couple is to have children for this is one of the purposes of marriage.

On this point, let me also warn you not to judge those who don't have any children or who have only one child. You don't know the health situations in this marriage, and for you to poke your nose and prod is rude and none of your business. It could be a couple wants children, but God hasn't opened the woman's womb. You could hurt people deeply by intruding into this area. Likewise a couple who only has one child may have only had one child because of health reasons. These health reasons are not anyone else's business. This command is between the married couple and God, not between you and the married couple.

9. Marriage is till death.

When a couple gets married, they vow to each other that the only thing that will end their marriage is death. That is exactly what God intended. Matthew 19:5-6 says, *"And said, For this cause shall a man leave father and mother, and shall cleave to his wife: and they twain shall be one flesh? Wherefore they are no more twain, but one flesh. What therefore God hath joined together, let not man put asunder."* When a couple gets married, God intended that only death should end the marriage.

The purpose of every marriage is to exist till death parts them. Divorce is not to be an option in marriage. Working your problems out is the option. Nothing but death should ever end a marriage.

10. Spouses should be a team.

Though points in this chapter will be dealt with later on in the book, in order to understand the purpose of marriage we must be repetitive. God said in Genesis 2:24, *"...and they shall be one flesh."* Notice this is two people becoming one. This is a couple becoming a team, working together to fulfill the purpose of their marriage.

Until you become a team, your marriage will never fulfill the purpose of why God led you and your spouse together. God never intended your marriage to be a battleground; He intended it to be a couple working together as a team to fulfill God's purpose for their marriage.

When a marriage fulfills the purpose for which it was instituted, then it will be a happy institution. God intended your marriage to be happy, so follow His purpose for marriage and your marriage will be happy.

Chapter 2

Honey After the Honeymoon

One of the greatest battles that a couple will face in marriage will be to not let their familiarity with each other cause them to lose the sweet spirit they had at the beginning of their relationship. God intended for marriage to get better as the years progress. With the attack against marriage in our society, a couple will have to work at keeping their marriage sweet.

One of the events a couple looks forward to before marriage is the honeymoon immediately following their wedding. We often speak of how a couple is in the honeymoon stage of their marriage. To be quite honest with you, I don't believe that stage should ever end. When we talk about the honeymoon stage, many times we are commenting about how a couple are sweet with each other at the beginning of their marriage. They have that "lost in love" look in their eyes and a smile on their faces as they enjoy their first few months of marriage. A marriage should never lose the sweetness that a couple experiences in those first few months. The sweetness between a husband and wife should be practiced at all times to keep the honey in the marriage after the honeymoon is over.

A few years ago I was preaching in a church and an older gentleman was greeting people as they came into the church. He told me that he could always tell when a couple had only been married for a short amount of time. This statement intrigued me, so I asked him how he could discern this. He told me it was easy to see because those who had recently been married always walked into church holding hands, and those who had been married for awhile rarely held hands as they walked into the church. In the few weeks after that statement, I watched couples as they walked into church at my revival meetings. This man was exactly right. When I saw people who had been recently married, they always walked into church holding hands. Those who had been married for awhile walked in separately; not holding hands. How sad that it is that obvious that a couple has lost the honey after the honeymoon.

The Scriptures command us in Proverbs 5:18-20, *"Let thy fountain be blessed: and rejoice with the wife of thy youth. Let her be as the loving hind and pleasant roe; let her breasts satisfy thee at all times; and be thou ravished always with her love."* In this proverb, a father was teaching his son to always be taken with his wife. In other words, he was telling his son to be diligent to keep the sweetness in his marriage. Notice that he told his son to be *"...ravished always with her love."* The word *"ravished"* means "to be overwhelmed emotionally with somebody." This father was teaching his son the importance of always being madly in love with his wife. He was teaching him that he needed to keep the honey in his marriage, even when the honeymoon was over.

Those who have been married for any length of time will agree with me that it is easy to lose the sweetness in marriage. Familiarity with each other can cause you to take your spouse for granted, which will cause you to lose the honey or sweetness in your marriage. If anybody ought to be sweet with each other, it ought to be a husband and wife.

Listen, you married each other because you said you loved each other. Who better to treat in a sweet way than the person whom you love? I believe that if you are going to keep the honey in your marriage after the honeymoon is over, then

18

you are purposely going to have to do some things to keep that sweetness there. Let me give you several things that will help you to keep the honey after the honeymoon is over.

1. Kiss each other the first thing every morning.

One of the best ways to start your day off right with your spouse is to kiss. Listen, you're married, and you should make it a frequent habit to kiss each other. Too many times the only time a couple will kiss is when one wants to be intimate with the other. This ought not to be! Kissing your spouse first thing in the morning sets your mind to be sweet toward each other.

It amazes me that before a couple gets married, the parents and the preacher work hard at keeping them from kissing. Then, after the couple is married, the preacher has to work overtime to get that same couple to kiss.

If you are going to keep the sweetness in your marriage, then you need to learn to start your day out right with a good-morning kiss. You should not start out your days being at each other's throats because you're trying to get out the door to fulfill your daily obligations. You should make it a point to kiss each other on purpose. This will help to keep the honey in the marriage from the very start of each day.

2. Kiss each other when one gets home.

The first thing a couple ought to do when they have been apart all day is to kiss each other. Notice, we started our day out by kissing each other so that we could keep the honey in the marriage from the start of the day. Now, we want to keep the honey in the marriage for the rest of the night. I believe when one comes home and walks through the door that it is good for a couple to give a hello kiss.

I know that some who read this think that I am being a little ridiculous, but let's face it, before you were married you would have thought what I am saying would be normal. So what has changed your mindset? It doesn't take too much effort when one gets home to stop what you are doing for a minute or two and come over and kiss your spouse. Your purpose for doing this is to keep the honey after the honeymoon is over. When other activities become more important than a couple kissing each other, then our priorities are wrong.

Song of Solomon 1:2 says, *"Let him kiss me with the kisses of his mouth: for thy love is better than wine."* The couple in this verse kissed each other. Probably no book is better known for teaching how to keep the honey in the marriage than the book of Song of Solomon. God wanted us to see that it is good for a couple to kiss each other. Make sure you make it a habit to kiss your spouse to start off their day and also when they return home from work.

3. Say "Thank you" for the little things.

I think one area where many couples are lacking, is in the area of being thankful for the little things that each does for the other. Though what your spouse may do for you may be part of the duties they are responsible for around the house, it doesn't hurt you to thank them for doing their duties.

Husband, when was the last time you thanked your wife for the meal she cooked or for doing the laundry? Though you may think this is what she is supposed to do, you ought to have the courtesy to thank her for doing her task. A little "Thank you" as a display of appreciation for the work she does will go a long way in keeping the honey in your marriage.

Likewise I ask the wife, when was the last time you thanked your husband for the hard work he does around the house? When was the last time you thanked your husband for accomplishing something on your honey-do-list? When was the last time you verbally thanked your husband for making sure the bills are paid? Though this is his responsibility as a husband, he would appreciate it if you would say "Thank you."

Every little task that each spouse does should be appreciated with a verbal "Thank you." Whether it is ironing the clothes, taking out the trash, cooking the meal, keeping the car running smoothly or other little tasks that your spouse may do; don't let these things be done without a thank you. A "Thank you" for the little things will help to keep the honey in your marriage.

4. Write love notes to each other.

When my wife and I were dating I was already involved in the ministry as an evangelist. Because of the long distant relationship due to my ministry, we wrote letters to each other on a weekly basis. To this day we still write each other notes to help keep the honey in our marriage.

A little note written and placed in your husband's lunch box will help to keep the honey after the honeymoon is over. A little love note to your wife placed at the kitchen sink will cause your wife to realize you took time to love her by writing a short note.

Let's be careful about getting so busy that we forget to write each other little love notes. I know some who read this think they are beyond writing love notes, and the truth is you probably are. But if the truth were known, you are probably beyond the honey in your marriage as well.

If we are going to keep our marriages sweet, then we will have to work at it. Writing a little note will let your spouse know that you took some time to think about them. That you took time to think about them will help your spouse know that you are working hard at trying to keep the honey in your marriage.

5. Eat meals together.

In our fast-paced society, we have seen the decline of families who eat together. Many think that this is not that important, but I believe it is important because this is time for the family to spend with each other talking about their day. When I say that we should eat meals together, I am talking about the family sitting and eating together at the table.

The average family rarely eats together anymore. Mealtime has become a time where everybody fills their plate with food and goes and sits at a computer or watches TV. Then we wonder why we have lost the honey in our marriages.

Ladies, make the mealtime a special time by preparing a meal for the family to eat. Men, if your wife is going to take the initiative to cook a meal, then you need to make sure that you are home when the meal is ready. When it's time to eat, spend time with each other and don't answer your phones. This is a time for the members of the family to be reacquainted after being apart for the day, and this is an important part of keeping the honey in your marriage.

6. Text love notes to each other.

With today's technology, staying in touch with each other throughout the day is much easier. Take advantage of today's technology to help keep the honey in your marriage.

Many times I'll be sitting at an airport waiting to get on a flight when I receive a text from my wife telling me she loves me and is thinking about me. When she does this, it makes me feel that she is working at keeping the honey in our marriage.

Though you don't need to do this every hour on the hour, I do feel you could use today's technology to send a little love note to your spouse. If they are having a harder day than normal, then text or email a note to them letting them know that you love and appreciate them. When they have had something exciting happen and they call to tell you about it, then text them later on in the day to let them know you are happy for them. A love note to your spouse through a text message is another way we can work at keeping the honey in our marriage.

7. Support each other's endeavors.

I can't express enough the importance of this point. If you are going to have a marriage that is sweet, then you need to support the endeavors of your spouse. What a shame it is for you to be more interested in the endeavors of your children than your spouse. Don't get me wrong, I believe you should support your children's endeavors, but your spouse should **ALWAYS** take priority over your children.

Ladies, you were made to be the help meet for your husband. You should support the endeavors your husband is pursuing. Though you may not know everything about his endeavors, learn to be there for him and act interested when he is talking to you about his pursuits.

Men, whether or not your wife is supporting you in your endeavors, you should love your wife enough to support her when she is attempting a task. When a husband and wife support each others endeavors, they know that their spouse is interested in them and this will help to keep the honey in the marriage.

8. Hold hands in public and in private.

It is very important that people see you as husband and wife holding hands. There is something about a couple holding hands that expresses to everyone else that you are in love with each other.

Likewise, just as it is important to hold hands in public, it is also important to hold hands in private. When your spouse wants to hold your hand, you should **NEVER** reject them. Though you may not feel like holding their hand, you may one day regret not holding hands with your spouse. It's too late to hold hands once your spouse has passed away, so you better hold hands while they are alive. It's too late to express your love to your spouse after they have left and divorced you. It's better to display affection with each other now by holding hands than to regret it later on in life.

As a couple, it should be a habit to hold hands with each other. In the car, hold hands with each other. In the house, hold hands with each other. In public, hold hands with each other. You should never be preoccupied with other things or ashamed to hold hands with your spouse.

9. Say sweet things to each other.

A couple should constantly say sweet things to each other. On a regular basis throughout the day, be one who says, "I love you" to your spouse. Call your spouse by little names like "honey," "sweetie" or other affectionate names you may have for them.

By the way men, there is nothing wrong with being sweet with your wife. Being sweet to your wife is not unmanly. In fact, it takes a bigger man to be sweet to his wife than to treat her like a piece of dirt.

Each couple should have affectionate names for their spouse, and frequently use them as you talk to each other. This is done to keep the honey in the marriage. Never let a day go by without saying something sweet to your spouse.

10. Don't say degrading words to your spouse.

Be careful about calling your spouse "stupid" or "dumb." There is nothing sweet at all about doing this and

this is uncalled for at all times. If you want to keep your marriage sweet, then you should never let words come out of your mouth that degrade your spouse. Even though you may not mean it as such, it is a blow to your spouse and will hurt the spirit of your marriage. Not only will degrading words hurt the spirit of your marriage, they will certainly hinder you from keeping the honey in your marriage.

11. Ride together as much as possible.

Don't fall into the trap of always taking two cars to the same place. As a couple, go places **together**. This is why we call you a couple, because you do things **together**. Ride to church together. Go to the restaurant together. I know there are some times when you can't ride together, but as much as possible, make it a habit to always ride together.

12. Serve each other.

One of the best ways to keep the honey in your marriage is to serve your spouse. If you spend your life serving your spouse and trying to make them happy, never expecting them to serve you in return, you will find your marriage will have the sweetness that you desire. When both husband and wife serve each other, you will find a couple who have kept the honey in their marriage.

It will not be an easy task to keep the honey in your marriage after the honeymoon is over, but the work to keep it there is well worth the effort. Don't let the attacks of the world and the busyness of your schedule keep you from working hard at keeping the honey after the honeymoon is over. You will find marriage is more enjoyable when both husband and wife work together at keeping the honey after the honeymoon is over. Be careful not to lose the honey in your marriage! In fact, let's not let the honeymoon end!

"When you live to meet your spouses needs, then the only dissatisfaction you will ever have in your marriage will be with yourself."

Chapter 3

Likeminded

The key to success in any relationship is for both parties to become likeminded or to be on the same page. A relationship will not work when both sides are going different directions. God makes a statement in the form of a question in Amos 3:3 when He says, *"Can two walk together, except they be agreed?"* There is no way a relationship will succeed unless both parties involved are in agreement and are likeminded.

For instance, a sports team where the players are not on the same page will fail. Superstars don't win championships; teams win championships. When I make this statement, I think of the great basketball player, Michael Jordan. In his early years as a professional player he was certainly the greatest player in the league, but his great ability to play basketball did not win him a championship. It wasn't until he learned to involve the players around him that his team won six different championships.

Likewise, two people who go into business together will not succeed unless both are on the same page. Over and over again people go into business with those who have different philosophies of how to run a business and they end up failing. This happens because a business can't succeed unless both sides are on the same page.

The success of every relationship hinges on how well both parties involved work together. One of the best illustrations of this is a couple who have been married for several years. When you ask a question of a person who has been married for several years, they can begin to answer and their spouse can finish the answer because they have become one in their way of thinking. The longevity of their relationship has caused them to think like each other.

If a marriage is going to be successful, it is very important that both husband and wife become likeminded. A marriage will not work if the husband and wife are on different pages. They must become likeminded in order for the marriage to be successful.

Philippians 2:2-4 says, *"Fulfil ye my joy, that ye be likeminded, having the same love, being of one accord, of one mind. Let nothing be done through strife or vainglory; but in lowliness of mind let each esteem other better than themselves. Look not every man on his own things, but every man also on the things of others."* In these verses God is teaching us that if a relationship is going to be filled with joy, then those involved must become likeminded.

The word *"likeminded"* is two words in one. The word "like" means "to be similar, resembling or to look alike." In other words, when God tells us to be *"likeminded,"* He is telling us to have similar minds, or minds that look like or think like each other. The second word "minded" means "intention, purpose, design or opinion." In other words, being likeminded is having like intentions. It is having purposes that are alike. It is having like designs. Being likeminded is having like opinions. Literally, being likeminded is when both parties in the marriage are pulling together and going the same direction.

A marriage should not be a tug-of-war. A marriage ought to be a team pulling together for the same cause. Like God said in the verses above, a married couple ought to be likeminded. Your marriage will never be happy and successful until you become likeminded.

If being likeminded is so important to the success of a marriage, then how do we become likeminded? As you look at Philippians 2:2-4, God gives us a detailed outline of how to become likeminded. Let me show with this outline how you and your spouse can become likeminded.

First, God said the first step we must take in order to be likeminded is *"...having the same love..."* When God talks about *"...having the same love,"* He is teaching us that a couple must have the same agenda. A couple who has split agendas in their marriage will never succeed at being likeminded.

When you got married, you were to leave everything and cleave to each other. Genesis 2:24 says, *"Therefore shall a man leave his father and his mother, and shall cleave unto his wife: and they shall be one flesh."* You will not succeed at having the same agenda if you don't learn to leave everything else and cleave to each other.

In order to have the same agenda, both husband and wife must understand their role in marriage. As we will discuss later in this book, the role of the husband is to be the head of the home. If a husband does not fulfill his role of leading the home, then it will be virtually impossible to have the same agenda.

Furthermore, the role of the wife is to be a help meet for her husband. Though this statement is not politically correct, the whole purpose of why God created woman was to help the man she married to fulfill the purpose of why God created him. The whole agenda of the wife is to make sure she helps her husband.

One of the attacks against marriage has been the necessity of the lady working outside the home. When both husband and wife work to pay the bills, then it becomes natural that both want to succeed on their jobs. This creates a split agenda in the home because the woman is pursuing the success of her employment and not the success of her husband.

I would advise every couple to do everything in their power to make it possible for the wife to stay at home. If you must downsize your home in order to make this work, then I would do it. My wife and I have worked extra hard at making sure she is able to stay home. We both believe it is important for her to stay home if we are going to have one agenda in our marriage.

Second, if we are going to be likeminded then God says we must be of *"...one accord..."* Being of *"one accord"* means to have the same direction in our marriage. The word *"accord"* means "to be in agreement; having a harmony of minds." In other words, to be in one accord is to be like a symphony that plays in harmony.

Years ago as a young man, I ushered at a symphony orchestra. Before the orchestra started playing, each instrumentalist would practice and tune up their instrument. I remember the first time I heard this I thought they were going to be terrible because of how bad it sounded. But as soon as the conductor stood up and raised his arms, the musicians stopped and waited for his direction to start. At his signal the music began to play, and what harmony came out of this orchestra.

That is exactly how a marriage ought to be. A marriage that has the same direction is a marriage that is in harmony and makes sweet music for others to see. Just like the orchestra members worked together under the same direction to make sweet music, the marriage that is going the same direction will bring harmony to the home.

If you want to have a marriage that is likeminded, then you must be in harmony concerning your finances. Disharmony in the marriage will occur when you have one spouse who spends money while the other is trying to save money. Both must be in harmony concerning the saving and spending of money.

Ladies, don't spend too much money on all of your hobbies. If you were to look at all the money you have spent on your hobby, you will realize there is a lot of money you could have used for better things. You could just about stock a store with all the supplies you have purchased for your hobby. Be careful about spending all the time.

Likewise men, be careful about the money you spend on your hobby. I know quite often the woman gets the bad rap on this, but there are many men who are worse than their wives when it comes to spending money. Men, there comes a point when purchasing another gun is not a need. I know I'm treading on thin ice, but you can only shoot so many guns. After awhile it becomes a waste of money. There are men who spend a lot of money on their golf habit. You must learn to be careful with your finances for the sake of keeping harmony in your marriage.

I also believe you need to be in harmony in the area of child rearing. Both parents need to be of one accord concerning how they are going to discipline their children. It should never be that one spouse always tries to make the other spouse look like the mean ogre. Never say, "You wait until your...get's home." No, if your spouse will punish the child for something, then you ought to be on the same page and punish the child yourself.

Be in harmony in your ministries of the church. I believe that it is best for married couples to work in ministries together. My reason for saying this is because I want the couple to both have the same direction because this creates harmony. Ladies, be careful about letting your ministry take you away from helping your husband to be successful in his ministry. When you can't help your husband be successful in his ministry, then you have become too busy.

In order to be in harmony concerning the direction of your marriage, you must allow the same source to direct you. Both need to be students of the Scriptures. Both need to read the King James Bible. Both need to sit under the same preaching. Both need to have the same counselor. This is important because no two counselors will counsel alike. Decide together who you want to be the counselor of your marriage. Also, both need to attend the same church. You will never be in harmony in the direction of your marriage if you are allowing different sources to direct you. Having one source directing you both will keep you in one accord.

Third, in order to be likeminded we must be *"...of one mind."* Being of one mind is having the same plan or blueprint for your marriage. You can't build a successful marriage by having two different plans. Try building a house with two different sets of blueprints and see how that will go. Give both sets of blueprints to the construction crew and see what happens. You will have chaos, disharmony and fighting. This is why many couples struggle with getting along because they have two different plans of how to do things.

If you are going to be likeminded in your marriage, then you need to be of one mind and have one plan concerning what you are trying to accomplish with your children, marriage and ministries. If both spouses have different opinions of what they are trying accomplish in the rearing of their children, then you will have problems in your marriage. It is very important that you both agree on your goals for the children.

You should both be in agreement in what you're trying to accomplish in your lives and marriage. The direction for all of these should come from the Word of God. It should not be what we want our children to become, but what God wants our children to become. It should not be what we are trying to accomplish with our marriage and lives, but what God wants us to accomplish with our marriage and lives.

The problem with having one mind in marriage is that there are two minds in each marriage. That means if we are going to be of one mind, then someone is going to have to defer to the other.

Men, it wouldn't hurt you to ask your wife for her opinion on things before you make a decision. Your wife is not an idiot! You may say that I don't know your wife, and if I did then I would understand. Well, you are probably right, she is an idiot because she married you. If your wife is smart enough to marry you, then I believe she is smart enough for you to ask her advice before making decisions.

Ladies, when you and your husband disagree on what should be done, then you need to defer to your husband and follow his decision. Now when you do this, don't follow begrudgingly giving your "opinion" along the way. If you do this, you will train your husband never to lead. There are many men who have stopped making the decisions in the home because their wife always made it miserable for them when they made a decision, and they just don't want to go through it anymore. In order to be of one mind, then someone is going to have to defer to the other.

Fourth, if you are going to be likeminded in marriage, then you must not be concerned with who gets the credit for accomplishments. God said, "*Let nothing be done through strife or vainglory; but in lowliness of mind let each esteem other better than themselves.*"

You must always remember that you are a team. When one team member wins, they both win. The great college basketball coach John Wooden said, "It's amazing what can be accomplished when no one cares who gets the credit." You must remember that when one succeeds, both succeed together.

Stop trying to be the "best parent." Don't question your children about who is the better parent. You will not achieve being likeminded in your marriage by always trying to outdo your spouse as a parent. You are a team, and teams are not concerned with who gets the glory. If your goal is to turn out children who serve God, then you both succeed together when this is accomplished.

Most strife in a marriage is all about who gets the credit for the accomplishments. It should never bother you when your spouse gets more credit than you because you are on the same team. When they succeed, you succeed as well because you are on the same team.

Lastly, if you are going to be likeminded in your marriage then you must look to meet the needs of your spouse. God said to *"Look not every man on his own things, but every man also on the things of others."* If you are going to achieve being likeminded in your marriage, then you must live to meet the needs of your spouse.

Marriage should not be about what you get out of it, but what you can put into it. If your goal in marriage is to meet the needs of your spouse, then you will always be satisfied with your marriage. If you live for your spouse to meet **your** needs, then you will always be dissatisfied because you are living for self. Self is never satisfied, for when it gets what it wants it is never good enough.

When you live to meet your spouses needs, then the only dissatisfaction you will ever have in your marriage will be with yourself. The reason being is if you are living to meet your spouses needs and don't expect anything in return, then you can only be dissatisfied with yourself when you don't meet their needs.

The statement, "Everything always has to be about you, doesn't it?" only reveals that you think everything is about you and not your spouse. The reason I say this is because if

34

you are living to make your spouse happy, and everything is about them, then you will be happy because you are not looking to get anything out of the relationship.

When you live to meet your spouse's needs, then it will not matter to you what you get out of your marriage. This mentality must be lived in order to have a marriage that is likeminded.

As I previously stated, marriage should not be a tug-of-war. Marriage should be a team pulling together trying to accomplish the work of the LORD. When a marriage is likeminded and on the same page, then that marriage will be happy and accomplish great things for God.

"To be quite honest with you, I would rather kiss my wife than a golf club."

Chapter 4

Leave and Cleave

From childhood to your teenage years, you looked forward to the day when you would get married. A girl will purchase a hope chest, and fill it with things she wants to save for when she gets married. Young men will start thinking during their teenage years about meeting the "right one" and getting married. Even at a very young age, children will play like they are married because of the mystique that marriage has in their minds. God has placed inside of children the desire to get married.

One day you finally met Mr. or Miss right. You started dating them with the purpose of fulfilling your desire to get to know this wonderful person more. As you dated them, you thought about them all day and night. You would write love notes to each other and call each other every time you had a chance. You knew in your heart that this person whom you were dating was the one with whom you wanted to spend the rest of your life.

Finally, you made the final decision in your heart that you wanted to get married. You got engaged and spent months preparing for the day that you would leave your parents and become one with the one whom you would marry.

The day of your marriage finally came. With all the preparations you made to make that day the beginning of a wonderful life, you finally got married to the love of your life. For the first few months of your marriage nothing could separate you and your spouse. Without noticing it, little things began to start squeezing themselves in between you and your spouse. Now, that closeness that you once had is no longer there. Where before you would let nothing come between you and your spouse, the familiarity with each other has allowed things to squeeze in between you, and now there is a distance where closeness once used to be. This ought not to happen in any marriage. In fact, the Bible commands us not to let this happen.

Genesis 2:23-24 says, *"And Adam said, This is now bone of my bones, and flesh of my flesh: she shall be called Woman, because she was taken out of Man. Therefore shall a man leave his father and his mother, and shall cleave unto his wife: and they shall be one flesh."* God warns in these verses that you will have to watch so that you don't let things squeeze between you and your spouse. He warns that there are many things that will try to separate you and your spouse.

Three times in the Scriptures God commands us to leave and cleave. The word *"leave"* literally means to forsake. In other words, when you got married you chose to forsake family and the former life in order to cleave to your spouse. You were to forsake your parents to cleave to your spouse. You were to forsake your family to cleave to your spouse. You were to forsake the single life to cleave to your spouse. Just as God wanted you to cleave to these things before you were married, He now wants you to forsake them and cleave to your spouse.

When God says to *"cleave,"* He means that you should pull together tightly so that nothing can squeeze in between you and your spouse. God knew that one of Satan's attacks against your marriage would be to get things to squeeze between you and your spouse so that the closeness God intended for you to have would not be there. God is teaching

38

that you will have to purposely hold tight to your spouse so that nothing gets between you.

Let me illustrate. When I preach on the verses above and try to explain what leaving and cleaving is, I bring a married couple up and have them tightly interlock their arms. I tell people that a married couple must hold on so tight to each other that nothing can squeeze its way in between them. I then have their child try and squeeze between them to illustrate how even your children can cause you not to cleave to each other. With this couple holding tightly to each other, nothing can separate them because they are cleaving to each other.

This is what you and your spouse are to do in your marriage. You are to hold so tight to each other that nothing can get between you. You will have to purposely hold tight and guard yourselves so that neither thing nor person can squeeze and separate you and your spouse.

Let me give you some thoughts about these verses that will help you to accomplish leaving and cleaving.

1. The man should lead in the act of leaving and cleaving.

You will notice in the verse above that God addressed the man and then the woman. The reason being is because God expects the man to be the one who leads in the home. It should always be the husband who, by example, shows how to leave his family and the single life to cleave to his wife.

Men, whether or not your wife leaves and cleaves, you are to be an example of how to leave and cleave. You cannot wait for her to make the first move, for you are the leader in the home. It is your responsibility to show your wife that you are willing to forsake all for her. By the way, that is the vow you took when you got married.

2. The wife is to follow her husband's example.

Because God made the woman for the man, she must realize that her responsibility as a wife is to cleave to her husband. Though God addressed the husband in these verses, God had already set the principle for the wife to submit and follow her husband's leadership.

Ladies, let me remind you that you were made for your husband and not for your dad. Though you may have a great love for your dad, your husband should be the number one person in your life. He should never feel that he is taking second seat to your family. He should always be number one. You should serve your husband before you serve your family because he is your number one. He should never feel that you would do things for your dad or family before you would do things for him. If he ever feels this way, then you have failed.

Let me take this one step further, you should leave your family and former life and cleave to your husband whether or not he leaves and cleaves. Though the husband is responsible to lead in this area, it is still God's command to leave and cleave whether or not your spouse obeys.

3. You will purposely have to obey the command to leave and cleave.

This will not be an easy task. Quite the contrary, it will be a difficult task to accomplish. Each thing you do in life will compete with that position your spouse is supposed to hold. Therefore you must realize that you will have to pay attention to this area of your life and purposely cleave to your spouse.

The half-hearted effort to cleave to your spouse will allow people or things to squeeze between you. This effort to cleave will have to be a joint effort in order to accomplish the task of not allowing anything to squeeze between you.

4. It will take effort from both sides to succeed at cleaving to each other.

As I previously stated, cleaving requires effort from both husband and wife. You will never have the closeness that God intended for you to have without both the husband and wife working on cleaving to each other.

For you to have success in this area, it cannot be a one-sided effort. When only one tries to cleave to their spouse, they are not cleaving, but holding on to their spouse so they don't lose them. Cleaving is an action done by both sides. Holding on is an act of one side and means that something is slipping away. The closeness and happiness in your marriage will slip away if only one spouse is trying to cleave. The only way to successfully cleave is for both spouses to give a full effort to this thing of cleaving.

5. In order to leave and cleave, you must realize that your spouse is more important than any person or possession.

Remember the day you got married and how nothing was more important to you than your spouse? In order for cleaving to be successful, you must never forget the importance of your spouse. If you feel other things are more important to you than your spouse, then you are not cleaving to your spouse.

Listen, if you are going to live "Till death do us part," then you better realize the importance of your spouse. Everything that you think is important right now will eventually be gone when you get old. Once they are gone, the only thing you will have left is your spouse. If your spouse is going to be with you till death, then there is nothing more important than your spouse. Without making your spouse the most important thing in your life, you will never accomplish the task of leaving and cleaving.

6. The purpose of leaving and cleaving is so you can become one.

You will notice in Genesis 2:23-24 that the whole purpose why God wanted the husband and wife to leave and cleave is so that they could become one. God wanted them to become one in thought, action, and direction. The importance of leaving and cleaving is so that you become a team that can accomplish the tasks God has for the both of you.

In order to leave and cleave, you will have to burn some bridges and decide not to go back to some former things. Your goal in marriage is to become one, and this will not be accomplished without some bridges to the former life being burnt.

Now let me caution you about some things that you will have to carefully watch so they don't squeeze between you and your spouse.

1. Family

One of the biggest culprits that will squeeze between a couple is family. I know that you grew up with your parents and siblings and that you have a love for them because they are family, but when you got married you promised to forsake all and cleave to your spouse. That means you must forsake your family and cleave to your spouse.

Don't let your parents squeeze between you and your spouse. Though you may be close to your parents, they need to take a second seat to your spouse. Your spouse is more important than your father. Your spouse is more important than your mother. Your spouse **MUST** become the one whom you run to with heartaches and victories.

Ladies remember, when you married your husband his career became more important than your parents' career.

When you got married, you were to forsake the career of your father and cleave to the career of your husband. If a lady is not careful, she will make the heartbeat of her life the career of her father and not her husband. Your husband's career should be the number one ambition and focus of your life. What your husband does is more important than anything else.

If you must choose between your family and your spouse, always choose your spouse. Your family needs to know that you will choose your spouse over them every time. If you must, then you need to go to your family and tell them that you will choose your spouse over them if they continue to try and squeeze into your marriage. Don't make your spouse the one who has to go to your family and say this; you must be the one to do this for it will carry greater importance when coming from you.

2. Children

Surprisingly, this happens more often than you would think. Once you have that little child, you must guard that your child does not take the place your spouse is supposed to have. Your spouse always comes before any of your children.

My wife relayed a story to me of something she saw at a church years ago. She knew of a couple who before they had any children would always sit right next to each other in the car on their way to church. After they had children, my wife saw them coming to church on a regular basis with the wife in the back seat with the baby. It amazed my wife that a lady would think her baby was more important than her husband.

Your marriage will go on after your children are gone and married themselves. If you allow your children to come between you and your spouse, when they are gone you will have a gap in your relationship with your spouse. You won't know how to converse with your spouse as you should because you allowed your children to come between you. Never let any child, even if they are a sickly child, come between you and your spouse.

3. Job

This one seems to happen more with men than with ladies. Though in our present day with women working outside the home, this does happen with them as well. If you are not careful, you can become married to your job and your spouse will sit at home feeling as if they are second to your job.

Your purpose for working is to pay the bills. There are many ladies who are widows at home even though their husbands are still alive. What I mean by this is the husband leaves early for work, comes home late at night and rarely spends any time with his wife. I know the job is important, but when your job starts causing problems in your marriage, then you better get your priorities straight and make your spouse more important.

Let me say one other thing about this subject. Don't be so possessive of your spouse that you don't allow them to work as they should. There are some who always complain about their spouse working too much. Be careful that you don't become a possessive spouse who always complains because your spouse is working. There is a very fine line of balance between work and marriage.

4. Friends

We all have our friends, but we must always make sure that our best friend is our spouse. Be careful that you don't run around with friends so often that your spouse takes a second seat to them. Yes, we all have friends, but you must never allow your friends to squeeze between you and your spouse.

5. Hobbies

Here is one of those things that can squeeze between married couples without them noticing it. I am not against having a hobby, I have a couple of hobbies of my own, but I determined awhile back that my wife was more important to me than any hobby.

I like to golf, but I cut back on my golf time because I felt spending time with my wife was more important than a round of golf. As much as I travel, I would rather keep my marriage strong than have a good golf game. To be quite honest with you, I would rather kiss my wife than a golf club.

Be careful that you are not in separate rooms at night working on different hobbies. I believe nighttime is a good time for the family to be together. Though there is nothing wrong with your hobby, when it takes time away from your spouse, then your hobby has squeezed between you.

6. Single life

When you got married, you chose to forsake the single life for the married life. There are many couples who still want to enjoy the single life after they get married. You must realize that once you got married you forfeited the right to run around with your single friends.

Trying to go back and enjoy the pleasures of the single life after marriage can certainly cause a couple not to have the closeness they should. When you got married, you were to forsake the single life and embrace the married life. Be careful not to try and enjoy both lives, for this will only cause problems when you and your spouse try to cleave to each other.

Remember, God commanded us to leave all and cleave to our spouse. In your marriage, be careful that you don't let anything squeeze between you and your spouse.

Till Death Do Us Part
You should hold onto your spouse so tightly that **NOTHING** can squeeze in between.

Chapter 5

In-Laws Go Both Ways

Many times when a couple gets married they don't really realize all that is involved with being married. When you get married, you are also marrying into the family of your spouse. Whether or not you like it, this is a reality. In-laws are a part of marriage that can cause friction if not dealt with properly. You can't take your spouse without taking their family as well. You may think that it won't be an issue in your marriage, but if there is any friction at all with your in-laws before marriage, it will be magnified after marriage.

The jokes about in-laws are funny for a reason. Most jokes are funny because there is an element of truth in them. If everybody had great in-laws, then in-laws jokes wouldn't make any sense.

One of the worst things in marriage is having in-law problems. When you took the vow, "Till death do us part," you never realized that in-laws were the ones who might kill your marriage. Dealing with in-laws is a very tedious subject, and one that must be dealt with in every marriage.

I believe that you can have a good relationship with your in-laws if you will work at it. I can personally testify to the fact that having a good relationship with your in-laws is possible. I actually met my in-laws before I met my wife. I was single when I started traveling as an evangelist. Early on

I had an opportunity to travel to the Philippines to preach at a pastor's conference. While preaching there, I met my future father-in-law, Dr. Steve Heidenreich, who had been a missionary for several years at that time. It was through this meeting with him that I met my wife.

I can honestly say that I have never had one ounce of trouble with my in-laws. To this day, I have a very good relationship with my in-laws. In fact, when my in-laws moved back to the States, they didn't have a place to live, so they stayed in our house for about a year and a half. Later on when we moved to West Virginia, they lived with us again for another year and a half. During this time, we never had one instance when there were cross words or times of friction. For many, a situation like this would almost cause a divorce, but we decided to have a good relationship with each other. Yes, it takes work on both sides, but we have been successful at it, and we enjoy being around each other. I thank God that I not only have spiritual in-laws, but I also have a good relationship with them.

Getting along with in-laws takes good people skills. Though your spouse is married to you and loves you dearly, they still love their parents and family as well. To make the relationship with your in-laws work, you must have good people skills. If you have a poor relationship with your in-laws, it is in part due to your poor people skills. If you have a good relationship with your in-laws, then it has taken good people skills to accomplish this. You will never learn how to get along with in-laws if you have a hard time getting along with people. If there were any reason for you to work at getting good people skills, it would be so you can get along with your in-laws. If you can learn to get along with your in-laws, it will help your marriage immensely. A good relationship with the in-laws will certainly enhance your relationship with your spouse.

There are three sets of in-laws in the Scriptures that stand out. The first set of in-laws would be the relationship

48

between David and Saul. David's relationship with his father-in-law was very tenuous at best, though most of this had nothing to do with David. He constantly worked at getting along with his father-in-law. The one instance in this relationship that I admire the most is when Saul was trying to kill David, David's wife, Michal, defended her husband above her own father. Though she could have lost her life for doing this, she still saw the importance of defending her husband over siding with her father.

Though David had a strained relationship with his father-in-law, his relationship with his brother-in-law was second to none. In the Scriptures, there is no one who epitomizes a good friendship more than David and Jonathan. Throughout both of their lives, they worked together to keep a good relationship. Even after the death of Jonathan, David still worked at honoring his brother-in-law because of their good relationship.

Another in-law relationship I like to read about in the Scriptures is the relationship between Moses and Jethro. There is not too much written about their relationship other than we see that they both respected each other's opinions. Moses took the advice of his father-in-law in the area of leading the children of Israel. Moses was burning himself out by trying to do everything himself when his father-in-law taught him how to delegate authority. Their relationship was so good that Moses not only respected his advice, but also followed this advice.

One other in-law relationship we see in the Scriptures was between Jacob and Laban. Here was a relationship that started out good but ended up bad. When Jacob first started working for his father-in-law, they both had a great working relationship, but something happened in the relationship that ruined it in the end. I believe that competition is what ruined their relationship. This act of trying to one up each other ended up with them being at odds with each other.

Genesis 2:24 says, *"Therefore shall a man leave his father and his mother, and shall cleave unto his wife: and they shall be one flesh."* We have already discussed this verse regarding the importance of leaving and cleaving, but there is another part of this verse that is very important to a successful marriage.

Notice in this verse who you are leaving; father and mother. This Scripture is dealing with the in-law relationship. As important as it is to cleave to your spouse, it is just as important to leave your family. If you don't sever ties with your family, you are bound to have in-law problems.

Let me take the next few pages and discuss how to deal with your in-laws. Let me make this clear for you to understand, I am talking to married couples and their in-laws. This relationship will only be what it should be when both sides decide to make their relationship work.

1. Neither side of the family is perfect.

When you first got married, the in-law issue was not much of an issue. The longer that you are married, the more the ugly head of in-laws will poke its head up. Before you were married, you didn't know as much about your in-laws as you do now. Before you only knew them on the surface, and truthfully they didn't know you as well as they do now either. Now you know the good and bad about each other, and this can certainly destroy your relationship if you allow it to.

If you are not careful, you will allow in the mentality that your family is better than your in-laws. You must never allow this thought to continue. This thought will start to drive a wedge between you and your spouse because you can't hide a thought like this. Though you may think your spouse does not know how you feel about their family, they know because it comes out in your attitude.

Let me remind you that every family has its issues, including yours. There is no perfect family! If we were to look into your family, I am positive that we could find issues that are just as bad as your in-law's issues. For you to think that your family is better than your spouse's family will only create a wedge in your marriage.

Remember that Romans 3:10 says, *"As it is written, There is none righteous, no not one."* Again in Romans 3:23 the Scriptures say, *"For all have sinned, and come short of the glory of God;"* According to these verses, even your family has sinned. This is why I say neither family is perfect, including yours. Don't allow the revelation of imperfections in your in-laws ruin your relationship with them.

2. Never criticize your in-laws.

One of the hardest things you will have to do is bite your tongue when you want to say what you think about your in-laws. Stating your mind is not always the right thing to do. Sometimes saying nothing is the best way to keep your relationship working right.

Criticizing your in-laws will not only cause you to have problems with them, but it will also cause problems between you and your spouse. You must remember that your spouse still loves their family. Though they may criticize their family, never join in on the criticism. Listen to your spouse, but don't say anything. When you start saying something about your in-laws, it will always come back to hurt your relationship with your spouse.

Proverbs 29:11 says, *"A fool uttereth all his mind; but a wise man keepeth it in till afterwards."* You don't have to say what you are thinking. The wisest statement you can make about your in-laws may be saying nothing at all. Whether or not it is true, never be critical of your in-laws.

3. Give equal time to both families.

Here is one of those areas that can cause problems without you saying anything negative. I have seen families who think they deserve the best part of the holidays over the in-laws. The best way to keep a good spirit and relationship with your in-laws is to establish early in your marriage that you will spend equal time with both families.

First of all, you and your spouse need to be the ones who decide with whom you will spend the holidays. You should never let your parents dictate to you when you will spend time with family during the holidays. This is not their business; this is now a decision to be made between you and your spouse.

Secondly, when deciding whom to spend time with, be just in your time with both families. Whatever amount of time you spend with one family you should spend with the other family. If you decide to spend Christmas with your family this year, then you should spend the next Christmas with the family of your spouse. This goes for eating meals at your in-laws, taking vacations together or just visiting each other. Always spend equal time with both sets of in-laws.

Lastly, when you are at your in-law's house, keep a good attitude, and don't show your displeasure when you have to visit. Participate in any activities that everyone does together, and don't be one who stays at home or in the hotel room while everyone else is involved in an activity. You can cause as many problems in your marriage by having a wrong attitude while visiting your in-laws as you can by not visiting them at all.

4. Deal with your family when in-law problems occur.

Unfortunately in-law problems do occur. When they occur and it is your family that is causing the problems, then you should be the one who deals with the issue. Never make your spouse be the one who has to deal with the problems. They already don't like your spouse at this point, and for you to make your spouse deal with the problem will only make the problem worse. You are making your spouse the "bad person" by making them deal with the issue.

I have found that when you deal with your family that it is best to relay to them that this is your feeling. Let your family know that your spouse is not making you handle the situation, but that you love your spouse and you will **NOT** allow family to ruin your marriage. If nothing else works when dealing with your family, then you will have to tell them if they force you to choose between your spouse and them that you will choose your spouse every time. Tell them you don't want it to come to this, but that you expect them to treat your spouse in a proper manner. Don't do this with a demanding spirit, but be sure you are firm in what you say. When you are done, then you will have to follow-up what you said with your actions. If you don't, then you will continue to have in-law problems.

5. Don't bring up marriage problems with your family.

Many times a spouse can cause in-law problems by telling their parents or siblings the problems they are having in their marriage. This is one of the quickest ways to cause problems with in-laws. This will cause them to have a bad attitude towards your spouse, because they will think your spouse is not treating you well. Even if you resolve the problems with your spouse, the feelings you created by revealing your marriage problems can go on for years.

You need to make it a practice to never reveal any private matters to your parents or siblings. This is not their business. Your family should never hear you talk bad about your spouse. They should only hear good coming from your lips every time you talk about your spouse. If you think your problems are bad enough to tell someone, then you need to seek counsel from your pastor. Always keep private matters private. Keep your relationship with your spouse a private matter, especially in front of family.

6. Spend equally on both families for the holidays.

Let me say first of all that what you spend on each other's families should be kept between you and your spouse. This is not something that should be discussed, even with your children. When it comes to deciding how much you are going to spend on your family, you need to be just in your treatment of each family. If you spend a certain amount on your parents, then you need to spend the same amount on the parents of your spouse.

Even if you have a strained relationship with your in-laws, be sure to treat them the same way you would treat your family. Don't hold back on how much you spend on your in-laws just because you don't get along with them. One of the best ways to overcome in-law problems is to follow the advice from Romans 12:21 when it says, *"Be not overcome of evil, but overcome evil with good."* Spending equally on both families will give you a better chance of working through your problems than if you spend more on your family.

7. Don't allow your parents to meddle in the rearing of your children.

In Ephesians 6:4, the responsibility of rearing children is given to the parents, not the grandparents. Therefore, you must quickly stop your parents from interfering with how you rear your children.

Your parents will not always agree with how you raise your children, therefore, when they start trying to meddle, you are going to have to quickly put a stop to it or suffer the consequences. If this happens, simply ask your parents to respect your decisions. Remind them that they did not always do everything right, but you still turned out fine, and that you will learn to be a better parent as time goes on, just like they did. Meddling in-laws will hurt your marriage.

8. Avoid giving opinions to your in-laws.

You can get yourself in a heap of trouble when you start shoveling out your opinion to your in-laws. More than anything else, our own mouths are what cause in-law problems. Avoid giving your opinion in areas that are sure to bring strife and contention.

For instance, if you and your in-laws believe differently concerning politics, then you would be wise not to talk about politics. If you disagree on religion, again you would be wise not to give your opinion about their religion. You can pray for them, and ask God to give you the right opportunity to witness to them, but don't make it a common occurrence that you always bring up your disagreements about religion or politics. Sometimes you will just have to agree to disagree so you don't create in-law problems.

9. Deal with in-law problems immediately.

Whenever you have problems with your in-laws, it is better to deal with the problem than to let it fester and destroy a good relationship. When I say deal with it, the first person you deal with is yourself. Make sure you are right. Then ask God to intervene and solve the problem. Lastly, if it continues to cause a problem, then you must sit down with them and politely, respectfully and firmly settle the problems.

10. Get counsel to settle in-law issues.

Sometimes the only way you can settle an issue you have with in-laws is to get counsel to help you through the problem. Counseling allows an outside person who has no feelings invested in the issue the opportunity to show you the best way to handle the problem. Proverbs 11:14 says,

"Where no counsel is, the people fall: but in the multitude of counselors there is safety."

Without counsel, your relationship with your in-laws is sure to fail, but with counseling you can make it work. I have always found that my pastor is the best person to get marriage help from, and this would also include my relationship with my in-laws.

11. Don't do business with in-laws.

One way to be sure to have in-law problems is to go into business with them. You may have a good relationship now, but you will end up having a bad relationship later. If you don't believe me, look at the relationship of David and Saul who were technically in business with each other. Business dealings with in-laws fail most of the time and will strain your relationship for years to come.

When I talk about business dealings, I am saying don't borrow money from in-laws. I know there are some for whom this has worked, but I have found that most people don't have the character to treat loaned money from in-laws with the same importance as they do their mortgage payment. Do everything you can to stay away from borrowing money from your in-laws.

You should also be very careful about going into business with your in-laws. This rarely works, and you are most likely not going to be the exception to the rule. If you think you know the problems of your in-laws now, when you go into business together you will find the problems magnify because now they are dealing with your livelihood. If you do decide to go into business, do it with much counsel. Be sure to have everything from the structure of the business to the details of each party's duties written out. Then expect that you will have to do everything yourself with them still getting the same benefits as if they were fulfilling their duties.

In-laws are one part of marriage that you cannot avoid. Work hard at having a good relationship with your in-laws. I believe that a good relationship with your in-laws is beneficial to your marriage and is worth the struggle to achieve. Make it your goal to sincerely thank God for your in-laws and the relationship you have with them.

"Two ingredients for a successful marriage are forgiveness and restoration."

Chapter 6

Divorce Is Not an Option

When a couple gets married, their hope and goal is to be happily married for the rest of their lives. Many people look for the right person with the plan to be married to them for the remainder of their lives. I would imagine that nobody goes into a marriage knowing that they are going to get divorced. If they knew this, they probably wouldn't get married in the first place.

Unfortunately, divorce has become all too common in our day. The percentage of marriages that end in divorce is nearly 50%. Of course, this number does not represent those who live together. If you were to factor in the number of people who live together as if they were a married couple, to the number of those who end up divorced, most likely the numbers would be much higher.

Too many people run to divorce when they want out of a marriage relationship. Sad to say that many people change their marriage like people change their bath water. Hollywood is well known for their divorces. Far too many Hollywood marriages end in divorce, and most stars end up getting remarried several times over. It's sad when a married couple in Hollywood are considered rare because they have never been divorced. This should not be rare; this should be common.

It is sad that our society has looked to Hollywood to define what a happy marriage is when they are the worst ones to whom we should look. Why would we look to those who can't keep their marriages together as an example of what a happy marriage should be? Instead of looking at the failures, we ought to look at those who have honored their marriage vows.

At the time of this writing, my grandparents, Pete and Florence Domelle, have been married for 71 years. Now there is a lot that must happen in order for a marriage to last this long. First, both must live to a very old age in order to be married for 71 years. Secondly, both must know the value of keeping their word. Thirdly, both must learn how to work with each other in order to make their marriage work. Seventy-one years is a long time to be married!

Every time I get around my grandfather, I tell him how honored I am to be related to him and my grandmother. I always tell him I want to shake his hand so that the longevity of their marriage can rub off on me. Whenever I say this to him, he always responds by telling me that their marriage has not always been easy. He told me that there were times at the beginning of their marriage when they struggled to get along. He then told me that divorce was never an option to them. He said they made a vow to each other when they got married, and they intended to honor those vows. They have most certainly honored their vows! If you could see them together, they are a great illustration of what a happy marriage looks like.

When you got married, you made a vow to your spouse and to God. Let me remind you that part of those vows said for better or for worse, in sickness and in health, in poverty and in wealth, you would love them till death parted you. This was your word that you gave to the one whom you married. This vow was not made just to them, but this vow was made to God as well. When you married your spouse, you took a risk and said that you would stick with them through thick and thin. Though there are some who have gotten the "worse" end of their vows, divorce should never be an option. Divorce is against the Scriptures and God's plan for marriage. Let me show you several reasons why divorce is wrong.

1. You made a vow to God.

When you said your vows to your spouse, you not only vowed to them that you would stay married till death, but you also made a vow to God that you would stay married till death. Though at times you may wonder if you can keep your vow, the number one driving factor in keeping your vow should be that you made that vow to God.

Deuteronomy 23:31 says, *"When thou shalt vow a vow unto the LORD thy God, thou shalt not slack to pay it: for the LORD thy God will surely require it of thee; and it would be sin in thee."* Notice that God says when you make a vow to Him He will require you to keep it. In fact, God made it very clear that it would be better to never make a vow than to make a vow and not keep it. Let me briefly explain, God is saying that it would be better that you never get married, than for you to get married and not keep the vows of your marriage. Though this can cover vows in many areas, we are discussing the portion of your vows when you promised to stay married till death.

Furthermore, the Scriptures say in Ecclesiastes 5:4, *"When thou vowest a vow unto God, defer not to pay it; for he hath no pleasure in fools: pay that which thou hast vowed."* There are two words in this verse that are very important, *"pleasure"* and *"fools."* God says when a person doesn't keep their vow to Him; they are a fool in whom He will not delight. God is literally telling us we are a fool not to keep our marriage vows. Yes, at times keeping those vows may be hard, but the best days of marriage will come if you will simply stick with it.

2. You gave your word.

Let me remind you that on the day of your wedding you gave your word to your spouse. You told them that no matter what your marriage may bring, you would stay with them, "Till death do us part." When you don't honor your vows, you are lying to God and to your spouse.

God commands us in Leviticus 19:11, *"Ye shall not steal, neither deal falsely, neither lie one to another."* Notice that God commanded us to never lie to each other. Again the Scriptures teach us in Colossians 3:9, *"Lie not one to another, seeing that ye have put off the old man with his deeds;"* God is teaching us that lying is a part of our old man before we got saved. Now that we are saved, we are to tell the truth all of the time. Even if you got married before you were saved, you are still required to keep your vows of marriage because you gave your word.

3. Divorce goes against God's plan.

God's plan for marriage is plainly described in Matthew 19:6 when it says, *"Wherefore they are no more twain, but one flesh. What therefore God hath joined together, let not man put asunder."* Notice that the plan is to be joined together and that no man should divide a marriage. To make this very simple, if you are a human being, then God says that neither you, your spouse or a judge has any right to grant a divorce, for that goes against the plan of God.

God intended that a married couple become one in marriage. They should become one in thought and action and in a literal sense, they become one unit in God's eyes. According to the Scriptures, once two people are joined together in marriage, it is wrong for anybody to end that marriage.

4. Divorce is a denial of the power of God.

Looking again at Matthew 19:6, God said that when a couple gets married they are joined together by Him. When God joins a couple, He intends for them to never be divided again, unless divided by death. Only God should have the right to divide what He has joined, and the only way He divides a couple is through death.

For someone to get divorced, they are denying that God has the power to keep them together as one unit. If God has the power to join a couple in marriage, then God also has the power to keep that couple married. When you make divorce an option in your marriage, you are denying God's power to keep your marriage together. Denying God's power through divorce is wrong.

5. God commands that death is the only thing that should end a marriage.

God shows us in 1 Corinthians 7:39, that the only thing that should end a marriage is death, *"The wife is bound by the law as long as her husband liveth; but if her husband be dead, she is at liberty to be married to whom she will; only in the Lord."* Notice that a couple is bound by the law to stay married until one of them dies.

When a person gets divorced, they are breaking God's law for marriage. Though it may be legal based upon man's law to get divorced, God's laws are higher than man's laws. The law that God set up for marriage is that death is the only thing that should end a marriage. Anytime you break God's laws, you will always suffer adverse repercussions.

6. Divorce is wrong because charity never faileth.

The Scriptures teach us in 1 Corinthians 13:8, *"Charity never faileth..."* In other words, once you start loving someone you cannot end that love. I like to say that there is no off switch to love. Once you decide to love someone, you can never stop loving them.

One of the reasons divorce is wrong is because you will never be able to stop loving the one whom you loved before. If you get remarried, you will still have a love for the one whom you originally married. That type of love is only for the person you marry. It is not right to have a spousal love for two separate people. It is wrong for you to divorce someone, because charity never fails.

7. Divorce is wrong because it hurts your children.

Children always pay the highest price in a divorce. In a divorce, the children always get the bad end of the deal. In fact, they must live with the consequences of divorced parents for the rest of their lives. Though their parents may move on with their lives, the children will have to divide extra time between each parent in order to be just to everyone. This is wrong!

As parents we are commanded to take care of our children. 1 Timothy 5:8 says, *"But if any provide not for his own, and specially for those of his own house, he hath denied the faith, and is worse than an infidel."* Divorced parents cannot properly care for the needs of their children when they are divorced. Therefore, it is wrong for a couple to get divorced.

Divorce is wrong for several reasons. We should do everything we can to avoid getting a divorce. Since divorce is wrong, let me show you some options instead of divorce.

1. Settle before marriage that divorce will not be an option.

If you don't settle before you get married that divorce will never be an option in your marriage, then one day when your marriage is going through trying times it will become an option. If it is not settled that divorce will not be an option, then a couple will always keep divorce as a consideration.

Before my wife and I were married, we were clear with each other that divorce would never be an option for us. Because of this, when we have had disagreements, divorce is not an option to which we run. Though you may already be married, you need to settle with your spouse that divorce will never be an option for your marriage.

2. Work out your differences privately.

Let's be honest, you are going to have differences with your spouse. Because you are going to have differences, and you have already settled that divorce is not an option, then you need to sit down and privately work out the differences that you have with each other in an adult way. I'm not talking about yelling at each other. I'm talking about discussing how you can overcome your differences.

Matthew 18:15 says, *"Moreover if thy brother shall trespass against thee, go and tell him his fault between thee and him alone: if he shall hear thee, thou hast gained thy brother."* Notice that God says the first step you should take when you are having problems with someone is to privately go to them and try to work it out. This applies to your marriage as much as it does to your other relationships. Sit down and find out what has caused the problem, and then decided together how you can avoid this problem in the future.

3. Get counseling.

When trying to privately work out your marriage problems doesn't work, then your next step should be to get counsel. Though this may be embarrassing, it is better to be privately embarrassed than to be embarrassed publicly when you go through a divorce.

The Scriptures command us several times to get counsel for problems in our lives. Proverbs 11:14 says, *"Where no counsel is, the people fall: but in the multitude of counsellors there is safety."* Let me paraphrase this for you, "Where no counsel is, the marriage will fall." When having problems, don't be afraid to get counseling. Many times a godly counselor will have some solutions for your marriage problems that you have not thought about.

4. Forgiveness and restoration

Two ingredients for a successful marriage are forgiveness and restoration. There will be times in your marriage when your spouse will wrong you. This can cover many areas. If you're going to avoid divorce, then forgiveness and restoration must be a common exercise in your marriage.

God commands us to forgive each other in Ephesians 4:32 when He says, *"And be ye kind one to another, tenderhearted, forgiving one another, even as God for Christ's sake hath forgiven you."* Forgiveness is an act on your part. When your spouse has wronged you, they cannot forgive you for their wrong. You must be the one who forgives them.

God goes even further in this process in Galatians 6:1 when He says, *"Brethren, if a man be overtaken in a fault, ye which are spiritual, restore such an one in the spirit of meekness; considering thyself, lest thou also be tempted."* Notice that after we forgive a person, we are also commanded to restore them. Not one time are we told it's okay not to restore someone for something they have done to us. In every case, we are to forgive and restore. Though this process will take some time and help through counseling, it must be a part of every marriage in order to keep from getting a divorce.

5. Don't risk your life.

I put this point right after the previous point because I know there are times when a person's life is at risk because of an abusive spouse. Let me first of all say that if you are an abusive spouse, you are not much of a person. You need to get some help immediately. You should **NEVER** strike your spouse for any reason. Likewise, you should not verbally abuse your spouse. Neither of these have any place in any marriage.

Secondly, if your spouse is physically abusing you, my first piece of advice is to call the authorities. They are not only breaking civil laws, but they are also breaking God's laws. Don't stay with your spouse at the risk of your life. Nowhere in the Scriptures does it say it is wrong for you to separate from your spouse when your life is at risk. Divorce is still wrong in this situation, but you should not risk your life by staying with them.

6. Leave vengeance to God.

When your spouse does you wrong, your reaction should not be to get even with them. Romans 12:19 says, *"Dearly beloved, avenge not yourselves, but rather give place unto wrath: for it is written, Vengeance is mine; I will repay, saith the Lord."* God says that we should never try to get revenge with our spouse over something they have done. God can take care of them better than you can.

7. Do good to your spouse.

God teaches us in Romans 12:17, *"Recompense to no man evil for evil. Provide things honest in the sight of all men."* When your spouse does you wrong, you are not to react by doing them wrong. In fact, God tells us to do the opposite in Romans 12:20-21 when He says, *"Therefore if thine enemy hunger, feed him; if he thirst, give him drink: for in so doing thou shalt heap coals of fire on his head. Be not overcome of evil, but overcome evil with good."* God says the way to overcome wrong is by doing good.

When your spouse does not treat you right, divorce is not the option. Doing good is your responsibility. I'm not to do good because my spouse does good to me. I'm to do good because it's the right thing to do. By doing good to your spouse when they are not doing right, you will find your good will convict them more than your fighting back and filing for divorce.

8. Ask God to work on the heart of your spouse.

When you and your spouse have a problem with each other, don't try to change them. The only thing you can accomplish by this action is for them to throw up a wall to your attempts to change them. God says He is the One Who changes people from the inside in Philippians 2:13 when He says, *"For it is God which worketh in you both to will and to do of his good pleasure."* Notice that this verse says that God works in a person.

When I have a problem with my wife, I don't try to change her, I ask God to do the changing. My prayer to God when I feel that my wife needs to change something is for God to change whoever is wrong in that situation. I tell God if I'm wrong then change me, and if she is wrong then change her. I have found that God can do a better work on the heart than I can, and He can certainly work on the heart of your spouse better than you can.

9. Change yourself.

I have learned that I have no power to change my wife. In fact, I have learned that the only one I have the power to change is myself. Romans 14:12 teaches us that we are accountable for our actions and not the actions of our spouse. So instead of wasting my efforts on trying to change someone I have no power to change, I have learned to focus my efforts on the one whom I can change, and that is myself.

Stop trying to change your spouse and change yourself. You will never change your spouse because only God can do that. So, instead of wasting time and effort on trying to change your spouse, you need to focus on the one whom you can change, and that is yourself. Change the one whom you can change.

I know there are many who read this book who have already been divorced. Though you can't undo your divorce, from this point forward you can take these principles and apply them to your present marriage.

Though there are several things that could be said about each point, my purpose for this chapter is to get you to understand that divorce is not to be an option, but working out your problems is the option you should take. Instead of taking the easy way out and getting a divorce, find a way to work out your problems. I'm sure that there is an answer to your problems. If anything, God has the answer. Ask Him to help you work out the problems in your marriage.

You made a vow to your spouse and to God that death would be the only thing that would end your marriage. No matter how hard it may be, keep that vow. In the long run, you will be thankful that you worked out your problems.

"Your wife wants you to love her for who she is and not for what she can give you."

Chapter 7

Giving Your Wife Security

One of the subjects men like to hear preached on, though few preachers have the backbone to do it, is for the woman to submit to her husband. Quite often you will get a hearty "Amen" when you mention this subject in a sermon. What men don't understand about this subject is that one of the reasons why God gave the command for the wife to submit to her husband is because He created her with the need for security. God knew that a lady would have a need for security that only a husband can give.

Men, women think differently than you. I know this is quite a revelation! Most men are analytical thinkers whereas most women are emotional thinkers. Because ladies are emotional thinkers, they need someone who can give them security. Emotional thinkers rarely have an inward security because they live off of their emotions. This is not a knock against any lady; this is just a fact of life. Yes, there may be an exception to the rule, but on the majority most ladies are emotional thinkers who need their husbands to give them security.

One of the greatest ways a husband can create an atmosphere for a happy marriage is to give his wife the security she needs from him. If your wife lacks security, you will find her stepping out of the role that God intended for her in order to try and find that security. This is why it is very important for every husband to do his best to give his wife the security that she needs.

As always, the Scriptures will show every man how he can give his wife security. The commands in the Scriptures to the husband are not there just to create a bunch of rules; these commands are there to help you give your wife the security that God knew only you could give her. Let me show you several ways the Scriptures teach how a husband can give his wife the security she needs.

1. Be the provider in the home.

God commands the husband in 1 Timothy 5:8, *"But if any provide not for his own, and specially for those of his own house, he hath denied the faith, and is worse than an infidel"* There are three words in this verse I want you to notice. The first word is *"provide"* and the second phrase is *"his own."* These are the key words to this whole verse. Notice that God was talking to the man when He said *"his own."* God was commanding the husband in this verse to be the provider for his family. In fact, God said the husband who doesn't provide for his family *"is worse than an infidel."*

Today's society has tried to turn this principle upside down. We live in a society where the wife is quickly becoming the provider in the home as the husband stays at home and cares for the children. This is completely against the Scriptures! I could care less what century we are in, God commanded the husband to be the provider in the home. Though at times the wife may have to work to help pay the bills, I believe it is still Scripturally correct for the husband to be the main provider for the family.

The husband should be the financial provider in every home. Your wife will never have the security she needs when you are not financially providing for her as God intended. It is not right that the wife must stress herself out trying to pay the bills because the husband is too lazy to fulfill his responsibility.

As a husband you should do everything in your power to be the one who financially provides for your family. This will provide security for your wife and bring peace to your home.

Furthermore, the husband is also to be the spiritual provider in the home. It is a sad day when the wife is more spiritual than the husband. Christianity is not for sissies! Christianity is for men! Jesus was a man, and a man who is going to be the proper provider will lead his home spiritually. I believe every husband should be more spiritual than his wife. Every husband should know more about the Scriptures than his wife does. Every husband should pray more than his wife does. Every husband should be the leader in his family's involvement at church. It should never be that the wife is involved in everything in the church, and the husband sits at home. Every husband should lead his wife and family in serving God in the church. If the husband is not leading his home spiritually, then he is not fulfilling his proper role as a husband.

2. Study your wife.

1 Peter 3:7 says, *"Likewise, ye husbands, dwell with them according to knowledge, giving honour unto the wife, as unto the weaker vessel, and as being heirs together of the grace of life; that your prayers be not hindered."* Notice that God commanded the husband to dwell with his wife *"according to knowledge."* The word *"knowledge"* in this verse means to make a science of your wife. In other words, study your wife so you know her ins and outs.

Study your wife's habits. As a husband you need to know the habits of your wife so you can better meet her needs. This means you need to be observant of your wife. For instance, study how she gets ready so you know not to interfere with her when she is getting ready to go somewhere. Though she may never say what time she will have supper ready, her cooking habit will help you to learn what time to get

73

home for supper. When you know the habits of your wife, it helps give her the security that you love her.

Study your wife's emotional patterns. Everybody has emotional patterns. We have our good days and our bad days, and it would be good to know when your wife will need some extra encouragement from you.

For instance, I know when I am very tired I can get a little grumpy. Because I know this about myself, I know I have to be extra careful not to be short with my wife and daughter when I'm tired. Just like I know my own emotional pattern, you could help your wife out immensely if you would learn her emotional patterns. If you learn her patterns, you will learn that there are some days when you might need to do a little extra for her to keep her spirit up. There might be other days when she won't be able to handle some of the pressures that life brings.

Study your wife's likes and dislikes. When your wife sees that you try to give her what she likes, it gives her a security that you love her, for you are willing to pay attention to what she likes and dislikes.

The best way to study your wife is to watch and listen. As she talks, if you will listen, you will learn more about her. If you will watch your wife, you will learn how to meet her needs just at the right time because you will have learned to make a science of knowing your wife.

3. Honor your wife.

Again I want you to read 1 Peter 3:7 as it says, *"Likewise, ye husbands, dwell with them according to knowledge, giving honour unto the wife, as unto the weaker vessel, and as being heirs together of the grace of life; that your prayers be not hindered."* Notice God commanded the husband to give honor to his wife. What God is teaching the husband in this phrase is that he needs to learn to treat his wife with dignity and respect.

Your wife is the queen of your home. If you want her to treat you like a king, then you should treat her like a queen. Your wife is not a maid or servant whom you order around. Your wife is the queen of your home, and you should learn to treat her with respect and dignity.

For instance, you should learn to always open the door for your wife. When she walks through a doorway, get in front of her and open the door for her. When she is going to get into the car, quickly get over to the car door and open it. This is an example of treating her with dignity and respect.

When your wife is carrying things, you should take those things out of her hands, and carry them for her. You should not make your wife a mule who carries all of your belongings. You are supposed to be a man who treats his wife with dignity and respect. When you carry things for your wife, you are honoring her.

One note to the wife: if your husband is trying to treat you with dignity and respect, let him. Don't make him sprint to the door because you are so quick to open it. Step aside and let him open the door for you. Don't be so quick to open your car door, give him a chance to do it. He is doing this because he is honoring you, and you should let him have that privilege whether or not you think it is necessary.

4. Love your wife.

The Scriptures command the husband in Colossians 3:19, *"Husbands, love your wives, and be not bitter against them."* This is an interesting command from God to the husband. You would think it would be normal for a man to love his wife, but God is talking about a deeper love than what the average husband gives his wife. God is talking about that "agape" love that is a deep abiding love.

Your wife wants you to love her for who she is and not for what she can give you. This is why God commands the husband to love his wife. It should never be that the only time you show appreciation and affection to your wife is when you want romance from her. Your wife should have confidence that you show her affection because you love her for who she is and not for what she can give you.

Love your wife by giving your life for her. Ephesians 5:25 teaches us that a husband is to love his wife to the same degree that God loved the church and gave His life for it. Your wife should feel that you love her more than anything or anyone else. You should not live for your job more than you do your wife. You should not live for your hobby more than you do your wife. She needs the security of knowing that after your love for Christ, she is number one in your life.

Love your wife by pampering her. In Ephesians 5:28, God commands the husband to love his wife like he loves his own body. God knew that men would take care of their bodies when they need attention. Likewise, you are to take care of your wife's physical needs by pampering her. When she wants a certain perfume or lotion, do everything you can to get that for her. By pampering your wife you give her a security that you sincerely care for her and love her. Don't be so gruff that you forget to show your wife that you can pamper her as she deserves.

5. Be the leader in the home.

1 Corinthians 11:3 says, *"But I would have you know, that the head of every man is Christ; and the head of the woman is the man; and the head of Christ is God."* Notice that God wants the husband to be the head of the home. God is teaching in this verse that the husband needs to be the decision maker in the home.

You will not give your wife security when you can't make decisions. No, decision making isn't always going to be easy, but God ordained that as the head of the home the husband is to make the decisions for the home.

Whether or not your wife will admit it, when you are the one who makes the decisions, you are giving her security. There is something about a man who has the backbone to make a decision that gives security to his wife. Don't waffle around on the decisions that need to be made in the home; just make them.

Be the decision maker about where you will go to church. Don't make your wife make the decision about whether or not your children should do something. You are to be the leader in the home which means you must make the decisions.

When your wife has to make decisions for the family, you are creating an insecurity in your wife. Yes, I believe it is good for you to get her advice and opinion on decisions that must be made, but you need to be the leader of the home and make the final decisions as to what will and will not be done in your home.

6. Guard her spirit.

I want you to notice the second part of Malachi 2:15 when it says, *"...Therefore take heed to your spirit, and let none deal treacherously against the wife of his youth."* Notice that God warns about guarding your spirit by not destroying your wife's spirit. The reason being is because God knows that if your wife's spirit is destroyed, then you will have a hard time having a good spirit yourself.

As the husband, I know there are times you might be tempted to dump everything on your wife, but your wife cannot take a constant dumping of all the negative that you face. The reason why God allowed you to face whatever you are facing is because He felt that you could handle it. The quickest way to destroy your wife's spirit is to constantly tell her all the negative that has happened to you.

When you come home from work, don't unload on her. Be very careful about talking about your disagreements with your pastor or your church. You will destroy her spirit and in return she will destroy yours. Many people have left a good church and pastor because the husband dumped the negative on his wife and destroyed his wife's spirit.

There are rough times when a husband will need the comfort of his wife, but these should be very rare occasions. You won't give your wife much security by being too weak to bear the brunt of the negatives that life brings.

7. Have fun with your wife.

Ecclesiastes 9:9 says, *"Live joyfully with the wife whom thou lovest all the days of the life of thy vanity, which he hath given thee under the sun, all the days of thy vanity: for that is thy portion in this life, and in thy labour which thou takest under the sun."* Here God is commanding the husband to have fun with his wife.

Marriage is more than just romance. Your wife needs to know that you can have fun and laugh with her. You need to be sure that you plan times to have fun with your wife. Yes, working together will create a close bond between the two of you, but she needs the security of knowing that you can also have fun with her. When you have fun with her, this gives her the feeling that she is not simply a tool that is used to fulfill your physical desires. Your wife should be your best friend, and best friends will both work and have fun together.

8. Make her your sole love.

Proverbs 5:15 says, *"Drink waters out of thine own cistern, and running waters out of thine own well."* God goes further to explain what He is talking about in Proverbs 5:18 when He says, *"Let thy fountain be blessed: and rejoice with the wife of thy youth."* God is teaching the husband that the only woman in his life should be his wife.

Your best friend should be your wife. There should be no other woman in your life and no other person in your life whom you would rather be with. Too many times men are looking outside of their marriage for happiness when happiness can be found by making your wife your sole love.

When your wife believes that you only have eyes for her, this will create in her a security that she needs. You shouldn't be looking at women who are dressed indecently on TV, the Internet or in magazines. Your wife should feel that she is the sole love of your life. Your wife should know that you want no one other than her. Enjoy your wife for who and what she is. Stop comparing her to other women. Your wife should never feel that you would want another woman, for you should make her feel that she is the only one whom you want in life. She shouldn't have to compete with another woman; you should be faithful to your wife. Don't be guilty of having eyes for someone else. Make your wife the love of your life. This is your choice! This is your decision!

9. Chase your wife to win her.

The Scriptures say in Song of Solomon 1:4, *"Draw me, we will run after thee: the king hath brought me into his chambers: we will be glad and rejoice in thee, we will remember thy love more than wine: the upright love thee."* Notice that this couple was running after each other. They were pursuing each other as if they were trying to win each other on a daily basis.

Remember when you were dating how you tried to win the heart of your wife? Remember the extremes to which you would go just to try and win her heart so you could marry her? If you want to give your wife the security she needs, then you daily need to try and win her heart. Don't fall for the philosophy that you are married and you don't need to win her heart any longer. Daily pursue the heart of your wife as if you were trying to win her over to you for the first time.

When a wife sees that her husband is still pursuing her heart on a daily basis, this creates a security in her that he is still madly in love with her. When she becomes the "old lady" who you no longer pursue and only put up with, then you will cause insecurity in your wife. You should make it a life long pursuit to win the heart of your wife just as if you were trying to get her to notice you for the very first time.

God created your wife with the need for you, as her husband, to make her secure. When a wife is secure in her husband's love, then you will find a wife who will want to please her husband in all areas of life. When a wife is secure with her husband's love, she will want to submit to him. It is up to the husband to make his wife the best wife she can be, and he can do this by loving her. When a husband loves his wife, she will feel secure with his love and will do whatever she can to please him.

Chapter 8

The Missing Piece

Genesis 2:18, *"And the LORD God said, It is not good that the man should be alone; I will make him an help meet for him."*

Every once in awhile our family will put a puzzle together. When I was a boy we would do big puzzles, but to be honest with you, I never have had the patience to do those big puzzles. So now, my family does puzzles that are a bit smaller than what we did when I was a child.

One of the most annoying things about putting a puzzle together is spending hours working on it only to have one piece missing. That one missing piece of the puzzle will literally ruin the puzzle. The puzzle is ruined because it is incomplete. It almost seems as if you have wasted your time when there is one piece missing.

A wife is very much like the missing puzzle piece in a man's life. Probably one of the most misunderstood roles today is the role of the woman. With the equal right groups pushing their agendas, the average woman has left the role that God made for her. According to the verse above, that role is to be the help meet for her man.

After God created the world and Adam, it was not long before God saw that man needed someone to help him accomplish the purpose for which God made him. Without the woman, man was an incomplete puzzle. Without woman, man would not be able to do what God made him to do. Therefore, God said that He would make *"...an help meet for him."* God's whole purpose for creating the woman was to help her husband.

When a wife does not fulfill this role of being the *"help meet"* for her man, then she has become that missing puzzle piece in the life of her husband. Both she and her husband will be incomplete without her fulfilling her role.

The words *"help meet"* carry a very powerful definition that help us to define what the wife should be to her husband. The word *"help"* means, "to aid; to assist; to lend strength towards an effective purpose; to relieve; and to change for the better." The word *"meet"* means, "fit; suitable and best." In other words, when God made the woman, he made her to be an aid to assist her husband which in turn gives him strength to accomplish that for which God made him, thus making him a better person.

According to the Scriptures, God made the woman to be a personal assistant to her husband. She was made specifically, as a perfect fit, to make her husband into the man that God wanted him to be. What a very powerful role the woman plays in the life of a man! Though the equal rights groups do not like this, this is exactly the reason God made woman. A wife will not be happy until she completes her role of being the *"help meet"* for her husband, and likewise, the husband will never be exactly what he could be until his wife fulfills the role for which she was made.

Ladies, you hold the power to finish your husband. You hold the power to be that last piece of the puzzle in your husband's life. Because you have such great power, you must be very careful how you use that power. You should not abuse your power, but use it in the way God intended for you to use it.

In the Scriptures, there are a few examples of ladies who abused this power that God gave them. The abuse of this power led to some very tragic consequences that these ladies never saw coming.

The first lady I think of who abused her power and hurt her husband's life was Eve. One thing that is commonly overlooked in the story of Eve eating the fruit was that she took over the leadership role in the home. When you read the story in Genesis 3:1-7, you see that Eve began to lead Adam instead of Adam leading Eve. Eve stepped out of her role as the help meet for her husband and instead began to lead her husband. Eve's leading led to sin entering into the world. This act is still felt today, as we must deal with sin in our personal lives on a daily basis. Why? Because Eve stepped out of the role for which God made her, which led to devastating consequence for everyone.

The next lady in the Scriptures who comes to mind that stepped out of the role of being the help meet for her husband was Sarai. In Genesis 16:1, we learn that Sarai told Abram to go to their maid and have a child with her. Though Abram bears part of the blame for this sin because he should have told his wife he would not partake in such a sin, Sarai was the one who used her influence over her husband to cause him to sin. This act of Sarai stepping out of the role for which God made her led to Ishmael being born. This has literally led to thousands of people being killed because of the enmity between the Jews and Ishmael's descendants.

Another lady who stepped out of her role was Rebekah. Isaac had become an old man and was about to pass the blessing of the birthright to Esau. We learn in Genesis 27:6-10, that because Rebekah loved Jacob more than she loved Esau she came up with the deceptive act to trick her husband into blessing Jacob instead of Esau. She had no right to do this, for God gave this act to the father. She was in essence stepping out of her role as help meet to her husband. This act led to Jacob wasting several years of his life deceiving people and fighting with his brother, and all because Rebekah stepped out of her role as help meet.

Another lady whom I think about that most people would agree was definitely not fulfilling the role for which God made her was the wicked Jezebel. The life of Jezebel is well documented in the Book of 1 Kings. Jezebel stepped out of her role of being the help meet to Ahab by influencing him to commit many sins against God. She influenced him to worship Baal. She influenced him to kill Naboth. She influenced him to put a contract on Elijah's life. This woman was nothing less than evil. Jezebel stepping out of her role, caused a whole nation to leave God and go into sin which ultimately led to the destruction of that nation.

One lady whom I think about who did fulfill her role of being the help meet for her husband was Mary, the mother of Jesus. In herself, Mary has no saving power for mankind, but her decision to be the help meet for her husband allowed Jesus to grow up in a very stable home. There were plenty of times when she could have questioned her husband, but she understood her role as help meet.

Another lady who fulfilled her role of being the proper help meet for her husband was Abigail, the wife of Nabal. We learn about her in 1 Samuel 25. Her husband was a very hard-hearted man. Instead of trying to take the lead in her home, she submitted to him in spite of how bad of a man he was. God blessed her after her husband's death by allowing her to marry King David.

One last lady I would like to point out who fulfilled her role of being the help meet for her husband was Noah's wife. The Scriptures don't tell us anything about her, but I go to my personal experience to find out what she was like. Think with me about this, for one hundred years Noah preached that God was going to destroy the Earth. During this time, he built an ark while many mocked him and would not listen. During this entire time Noah's wife followed him, as she was one of the eight people who stepped into the ark. What a great lady! She helped her husband become the man that God wanted him to be when she could have worked against him because of how crazy his task seemed.

Many pages could be written about ladies in the Bible who did and did not fulfill their roles as the help meets for their husbands and the results of their actions. In spite of what present day society thinks about this, you will never be happy as a wife until you fulfill the role for which God made you, and that is to be your role as the help meet for your husband. Let me give you several thoughts concerning the wife's role of being the help meet to her husband.

1. Woman was made for man.

In 1 Corinthians 11:9, the Scriptures say, *"Neither was the man created for the woman; but the woman for the man."* Now I am not saying this, God is saying this in the Scriptures. God made it very plain for us to understand that man was not created for the woman, but the woman was created for the man.

You will never be happy in your life until you fulfill that role for which God made you. We are starting to see the effects of women leading in the home in all the dysfunctional children and families today. Many women today have left the work place to go back home and be the homemaker and rear the children. I believe the reason for this is because they realized they were happier when they were fulfilling the role for which God made them.

God did not create the man to follow the woman, but God created the woman to follow the man. I know this is a very unpopular statement, but until a wife gets back to fulfilling her role, she will never be happy. If you want to be happy as a wife, then you need to understand that you were made to be the help meet for your husband.

2. Each woman was made for a specific man.

Look again at Genesis 2:18 when it says, *"And the LORD God said, It is not good that the man should be alone; I will make him an help meet for him."* Notice that God said He would make a woman specifically for Adam. This was the pattern God would follow from that point forward.

You must realize that you were made specifically for your husband. Looking at the definition of being a help meet, we learned that the word *"meet"* means, "fit; suitable or best fit." In other words, you are the best fit for your husband. God tailor made you to be the best person to help your husband become what God wanted him to be. No other lady can help your husband become what he should be because God made you for him. Your whole purpose of existence is to be the help meet for your husband.

3. A woman's calling in life is to be the help meet for her husband.

Quite often while preaching in a meeting I will make a call for full-time service. It is not uncommon to see young ladies flock to the altar and surrender their lives to serve God full-time. I have counseled many ladies who feel that God has called them to be a missionary or pastor's wife.

Let me make this very plain and clear, the calling of God for a lady is to be a wife to her husband. God does not call a lady to be a missionary; he calls her to be a wife to the husband for which she was created. God does not call a lady to be a preacher's wife or evangelist's wife; God calls a lady to be the help meet to the husband for whom she was created.

I feel that we have confused this truth in our churches today. With the movement of women preachers and the equal rights groups, we think a lady is called to be something other than a wife, and according to Scripture, this is not true. When a lady surrenders to serve God full-time, she is surrendering to do whatever God has called her husband to do. Nothing more and nothing less!

4. You were created to be your husband's personal assistant.

When you take the Scriptures literally, which you should, you cannot disagree with this statement. I know I am treading on thin ice with those who have swallowed the world's philosophy, but God made the woman to assist her husband in becoming that for which God created him.

I truly believe that I could have never achieved what I have in my life without my wife. She has wonderfully fulfilled her role of being my personal assistant in the ministry. I have watched her go through hard times and never complain because she understands her role. She has never one time in our marriage ever complained about the ministry and how tough it is. Instead she has taken the role for which God made her and helped me, and continues to help me, to become the preacher God created me to be.

Ladies, until you decide to become your husband's personal assistant and stop balking every time he tries to do something for God, you will never be happy. You will only be happy when you do what you were created to do.

5. A woman out of her role will cause her puzzle to be incomplete.

Your family will never be what it should be until you decide to fulfill your role as the help meet. Your husband will never become the man he should be until you decide to fulfill your role as his help meet.

Ladies, you are the final piece to the puzzle of your husband and family. Don't cause their puzzle to be incomplete because you won't be the help meet.

God will not judge a woman by how high she climbed the corporate ladder. God will judge a lady by how good of a help meet she was to her husband. God will not judge a woman by what powerful position she held in political office. God will judge a lady by how well she fulfilled her role of being a help meet to her husband. Stop trying to measure up with the world's measuring stick and measure up to the scriptural measuring stick of what God created you to be. When you do this, you will find happiness and peace that the world will never understand. It is in fulfilling your role as a help meet where you will find the satisfaction that you desire in life.

6. A woman out of her role will cause frustration and confusion.

Let me go back to the puzzle analogy in order to clarify this point. You know how frustrating it is to have one piece missing in a puzzle that you have worked so hard on. Well that is what happens in a marriage when the wife won't be the help meet to her husband. She causes frustration in the marriage.

Furthermore, it will cause confusion in the marriage because anything out of God's divine order causes confusion. This is one of the reasons why children are so unstable today; they are confused. God places the proper order of how things should be run inside of every individual, and when those roles are not being fulfilled, then confusion sets in. Don't be guilty of allowing your children to grow up confused about the proper order in the home because you won't fulfill God's purpose for your life, which is to be the help meet to your husband.

7. Only a woman can complete the marriage puzzle.

I know this whole chapter goes against the empowerment movement for ladies. The fact of the matter is, a woman who realizes that she is the final piece to the puzzle of her marriage can realize she holds great power in her actions.

Ladies, you will either make or break your husband's success by whether or not you will be his help meet. You are the final piece to the puzzle of your husband's life. Don't misplace that piece by not fulfilling your role. You really don't want the responsibility of not allowing your husband to fulfill the role for which he was created.

Furthermore, don't abuse the power that God has given you; instead you should use it wisely. Power abused will hurt many, but power used properly will help many. You can take the power of being the help meet for your husband and use it to help him become the man God intended for him to be.

I have watched many ladies push their husbands out of God's calling for their life because it was not what they wanted. Don't be that type of wife! Realize you're the missing piece to the puzzle of his life. Place yourself where you are supposed to be and your marriage will paint a beautiful picture of what God intended.

"Ladies are more empowered when they practice submission than they are when they won't submit."

Chapter 9

Proper Roles in the Marriage

Understanding your position and role in your marriage, and properly executing that role will help you to avoid many of the obstacles that cause marriage problems. Many arguments in marriage can be avoided if each spouse will fulfill the role that God set up for them. As the case in any relationship, when someone is not fulfilling their role, it causes undo stress in that relationship. Likewise, when a husband or wife do not fulfill their role, then the other spouse can become frustrated which leads the couple to have arguments that could have been avoided if they would have just fulfilled their marital roles.

When I talk about your role in marriage, I am talking about your God given duty as a husband or wife. In every marriage, the husband and wife have a duty or job to fulfill. This duty is the role God set up for them. If you don't fulfill your role, then this will cause friction between you and your spouse. It is very important that both husband and wife fulfill their role in order to make the marriage work properly.

God says in Ephesians 5:23-25, *"For the husband is the head of the wife, even as Christ is the head of the church: and he is the saviour of the body. Therefore as the church is subject unto Christ, so let the wives be to their own husbands in every thing. Husbands, love your wives, even as Christ also loved the church, and gave himself for it;"* In these verses God gives us a very clear picture of the role that the husband and wife are to fulfill. These roles are not always going to be easy to fulfill, but it is your responsibility do your part. It would be wrong for your spouse to fulfill their role and for you to allow your role to go unfulfilled.

These roles that God commands in the Scriptures are not always going to be looked upon kindly by society. In fact, if you fulfill your role, society may think you are out of date and need to get caught up with the times. But, when you look at the marriages that society has produced and compare them to the marriages that the Scriptures have produced, you will see that society's marriages are dysfunctional. The marriages that follow the Scriptures are happy and filled with joy. Let me make a few statements about these roles and then describe the roles in marriage.

1. These roles are not a choice, but a command.

When you read Ephesians 5:23-25, you never see that God gives the husband and wife a choice to do anything differently. These verses are a command to both the husband and wife. When God commands us to do something, then we are to follow that command without question.

Imagine in the military a superior officer giving a command to a soldier, and the soldier telling the officer that they just don't see it in the same light. That soldier would find himself in a very uncomfortable position, for their role is to obey the commanding officer.

God is the commanding officer when it comes to our marriages. God is the One Who started the institution of marriage, and I would think He knows what is best for your marriage. You will be happier in your marriage when you understand that Ephesians 5:23-25 is a command, not a choice.

2. It will take work to fulfill your role in marriage.

Nobody ever said that marriage would be easy. Hollywood has portrayed to children that once you find the right person to marry then you will live happily ever after. Let me make this very clear, marriage is not a fairy tale. It is real life. In real life if a marriage is going to be successful, it takes hard work by both spouses.

It will take work to succeed in fulfilling your role in marriage, but it will be gratifying once you fulfill that role. You will find that your work to fulfill your role will be one of the best investments you can make.

3. It will take character to fulfill your role in marriage.

If you are going to fulfill your role, then you will have to have some character to succeed in that role. It will take character because there will be times when you won't feel like doing your job, but character will demand that you do your job. If you don't have character, then you will struggle to fulfill your role. Successful marriages are filled with people of character. If there is ever a reason to get character, it should be so that you can fulfill your role in your marriage, for that is what it will take.

4. It will take self-control to fulfill your role in marriage.

You will only be successful in fulfilling your role in marriage if you practice self-control. The reason I say this is because when you see your spouse not doing their part, you will be tempted to give in and not do your part. Of course character and self-control go hand in hand, but without self-control you will never succeed in the role you're to fulfill in your marriage.

5. You will have to purposely execute your role.

As I look at the roles God gives to the husband and wife, I realize that each role must be done on purpose. These roles

93

don't come naturally, for if they did God would not have to command us to do them. God knew when He gave the roles for the husband and wife that they would have to purposely execute those roles.

This is why you need character and self-control, for without these you will not execute your role. Any role in the marriage that God commands us to perform will have to be done on purpose; they will never be done by mistake.

Let me take the next few pages to show you the roles that God commands for the husband and wife. Let me make this clear, these roles that I will show are not what I think a husband and wife should do, these are the roles that God commands of the husband and wife.

THE HUSBAND

1. The husband is to be the head of the wife.

In every marriage, someone has to be in charge. You cannot have two people in charge, because that will never work. I have always said that something with two heads is a monster. I fear that many times we have swallowed the politically correct mentality that marriage is a co-leadership role. That is not what the Scriptures command. God very plainly states that the *"husband is the head of the wife."*

When God talks about the husband being the *"head of the wife,"* He means that the husband is the leader in the home. It comes down to the fact that one person must be in charge and lead the marriage and home in the direction that God wants them to go.

2. Being the head of the home does not make your wife a slave.

I am against this mentality that the wife is only good to make biscuits and have babies. The wife is not a slave that the husband has a right to boss around. Just because the husband is the head of the home does not mean that the wife is to be his slave.

In fact, as I will discuss a little later in this chapter, the opposite is true. The husband is not to sit in his lounge chair bossing his wife around while he sits there and does nothing. Men, being the head of the home actually means you will be more involved and not less involved. Being the head of the home does not make you a master, but simply the one who is held responsible by God for how your home serves Him and follows His commands.

3. Being the head of the home means you <u>must</u> be the decision maker.

This is where many men fail in our homes today. Many husbands want to push the decision-making off onto the wife, when it is their responsibility to make the final decision. It is always easier to make your wife make the final decision, but you are the head of the home and you need to be the decision maker.

Men, when your wife asks you what to do, don't respond back by saying, "Well, whatever you want to do." She just asked you to lead by making a decision, now make a decision. Your wife is trying to let you be the leader in the home when she asks for your decision, now fulfill your role and lead. When the children come to you and tell you that their mother told them to ask you what to do, then make a decision instead of telling them to do whatever their mother said to do. This is the reason you are the leader in the home; you must make decisions. Whether or not you like making decisions is not a factor. God commands you to be the head in the home, which means you must be the decision maker, so you must learn to make decisions and follow through with the decisions you've made.

4. God holds the husband accountable for how he leads.

Because it is the role of the husband to be the leader in the home, God holds him accountable for how he leads, not for how the wife follows. This is very important to understand because whether or not your wife does what she is supposed to do, you are still to fulfill your role as leader.

The leadership role that God gave to the husband was not dependent upon whether or not the wife does her part; the husband is to lead even if the wife does not want him to lead. God does not judge you as a husband by how good of a husband you are compared to other men, but by how you lead your wife.

5. The husband should lead in love.

Notice in verse 25 that God followed up with the command for the husband to be the head of the home by commanding the husband to also love his wife. This was no mistake by God!

Leadership that is controlled by a love for what it leads will cause leadership to lead properly. If the husband will lead out of love for his wife and not out of selfishness, then he will lead his wife and family down the right paths of life. It is when a husband leads by selfishness that he only does what he wants to do. But, when a husband leads by love, then he will lead his family in the paths that God wants the family to go in knowing that those paths will lead to happiness. Proper leadership by the husband is done in love.

6. Being the leader makes the husband a servant.

Notice again in verse 25 that the husband is to lead by giving himself to his wife. As a leader, you don't lead by demanding people follow you; you lead by serving those whom you lead.

The husband who wants his wife to follow him will serve his wife. Remember where I said that being the head of the home doesn't make your wife your slave? In fact, being the head of the home means you will serve your wife and try to meet her needs. This is what leadership does. Leadership leads by example. Leadership that leads by serving leaves a great example for their followers to follow.

7. As the head of the home, the husband should lead in all matters.

Husbands, as the head of the home you should lead your wife spiritually. It should never be the case that your wife is more spiritual in any area than you are. You are the leader. You should lead your wife and family to go to church by going to church yourself. You should lead your wife and family to be soul winners by being a soul winner yourself. Likewise, the same can be said about honesty, character, prayer, Bible reading, knowledge of the Scriptures, etc. As the head of the home, you should be the one who leads in every matter, not your wife.

THE WIFE

1. The wife is to submit to the husband's leadership.

I know this is a very unpopular subject in today's society, but the fact is that God still commands the wife to submit to her husband. One of the greatest problems in the home today is the wife not submitting to the husband. The equal rights movement has been pushed for decades, and we have allowed that mentality to creep into our Christian homes which is dead against the Scriptures.

Ephesians 5:22 says, *"Wives, submit yourselves unto your own husbands, as unto the Lord."* The word *"submit"* means, "to yield or surrender your power." When God commanded the wife to submit to the husband, He was commanding her to yield to her husband's leadership. God is commanding the wife to surrender her power over to her husband so that he can be the leader that he should be.

I want you to notice that God dealt with the wife first and the husband second. The reason why is because your husband cannot lead if you won't submit. He can try all he wants to lead in your marriage, but unless you allow him to lead he cannot lead. Ladies, the degree that your husband can lead is dependent upon the degree that you submit to your husband.

2. Submitting does not make you second-rate.

Though our present society tries to make it sound as if a woman is second-rate if she submits to her husband, the opposite is true. When a wife is willing to submit to her husband, she is showing that she cares enough for her marriage that she is willing to surrender her power so that he can lead. This action will stop most of the friction in a marriage.

Ladies, when you submit you are fulfilling a role that no man could ever fill. Someone must lead in the home, and God chose man to be that leader, then that means the wife must submit in order for the husband to lead. If the truth were known, great husbands are only great because their wives have allowed them to be great by submitting to them. Abraham would not have been a great man of faith without Sarah submitting to his leadership. Noah would not have been a stalwart of standing for truth without his wife standing behind him and allowing him to take that stand in spite of their society. Likewise, your husband cannot be the man God intended for him to be without you submitting to him and allowing him to reach God's intended potential for him. Always remember, behind every great man is a great wife who allows him to be the man he is.

3. Submitting is giving in to your husband when you have the power not to do what he wants you to do.

True submission is not doing what you want to do when you are asked to do it. True submission is surrendering your will and following your husband when you don't want to do something, and have the power not to do it. If you were going to do what your husband asked you to do anyway, then that is not submission. Submission is when your husband asks you to do something and you don't want to do it, but you do it anyway.

Likewise, true submission does not give its opinion after the decision to lead has been made. Ladies, allow your husband to make decisions without always having to give your two cents. Many times a wife will do what her husband asks her to do, but she gives her mind of disagreement while doing it. Submission is as much an attitude as it is action. If you submit in action, but not in attitude, then you are not submitting.

Furthermore, true submission doesn't always make your husband pay by putting up with your attitude. Ladies, you know what I am talking about when I say this. Your husband makes a decision, and you follow him, but he has to put up with your attitude the whole time. This is not submission! If you are not careful, you will give your attitude one too many times and your husband will get tired of leading, because every time he does, he has to put up with your attitude. You may win the battle to get what you want, but you will lose the war and end up with a husband who will not lead. Submission is doing what you are asked to do, when you don't want to do it and have the power not to do it, and doing it with a good attitude. That is true submission.

4. True submission shows true power.

Ladies, it takes more power to submit to your husband than to get your own way. Though the equal rights crowd may say that submitting puts ladies back into the Dark Ages, the opposite is true. When a lady goes against her own will and attitude to follow her husband, this shows great power.

Ladies are more empowered when they practice submission than they are when they won't submit. When a husband knows that his wife will do whatever he asks her to do, this puts pressure on him to be sure that he is properly leading.

5. Your submission to your husband shows your submission to God.

God is the One Who commands the wife to submit to her husband. The degree to which she submits to her husband shows the degree to which she obeys and submits to God. You cannot be a good Christian wife unless you submit to your husband. The more you submit yourself to your husband's leadership, the greater Christian you will become.

I don't care how much you do in your church; if you won't follow your husband's leadership then you are a bad Christian. This idea that being heavily involved in the church makes you a good Christian is not what God looks at; God looks at how you follow your husband. That means that as he leads you spiritually, you will be involved in the LORD's work because your husband will lead you to do this.

Your marriage will be successful in accomplishing God's will to whatever degree both husband and wife fulfill their marriage roles. You will find that when the husband and wife fulfill their roles, there will be less strife in the marriage. Work on fulfilling your role in your marriage and watch the degree of happiness and enjoyment increase. You will never enjoy your marriage the way God wants you to enjoy it until you fulfill the role He commands you to fill.

Chapter 10

Finances

Finances is one of the three main reasons that marriages end in divorce. Other than infidelity, finances cause more stress on the marriage relationship than anything else. If you want to keep your marriage stress free and happy, then you will have to work on keeping your finances in order.

Proverbs 19:4 says, *"Wealth maketh many friends; but the poor is separated from his neighbour."* Notice that you will find friendship in wealth and separation from those whom you love when you are poor. Being wealthy and poor is a relative term in that a person is wealthy when their "wants" meets their "haves." Just because a person has a lot of money does not make them wealthy. There are plenty of wealthy people who have so much debt that they are actually poor. Likewise, I have seen people who have little money, but are wealthy because they don't want more than they have.

Your marriage cannot be happy when you are struggling with your finances. When you have the bill collectors calling every night trying to get their money, you will find your marriage filled with stress, which eventually will lead to strife. One of the best ways to help keep your marriage stress free is by keeping your finances in proper order. It is better to start by keeping your finances straight when you first get married, but there are many who will read this book who have been married for quite some time whose finances are in trouble. You have to start somewhere, so whichever situation you find yourself in, start working on keeping your finances in good condition from this point forward.

In the next few pages I want to give you several suggestions that will help you to keep your finances in good working order. Of course, there is no way that one chapter in a book can properly deal with all financial areas, but I will give you some guidelines regarding finances that will help you to keep them in proper order. You will find that your marriage will be much stronger if you keep your finances in good condition.

1. Live by a budget.

Proverbs 27:23-24 says, *"Be thou diligent to know the state of thy flocks, and look well to thy herds. For riches are not for ever: and doth the crown endure to every generation?"* In the Scriptures, many people measured their wealth by the size of their flocks and herds. God commanded us to *"know the state of thy flocks, and look well to thy herds."* A shepherd who didn't know the size of his flocks or herds was destined to lose money. With a budget and inventory of his herds, and knowing when to buy and sell, he could keep his flocks and herds growing.

Likewise, when a couple lives by a budget, they will find that they will have more money to spend in the long run. A family without a budget is a family that will never have money. Your budget should be the boss of your money. You must let your budget dictate what you can and cannot spend. If your budget is not your financial boss, then you will always find yourself short of money. It's amazing how much we can spend when we don't have a budget. Just a little here and there will cause you to lose money. This is why you must set up a budget. If you don't know how to set one up, then get with someone who can teach you. If you will sacrifice now by setting up and living by a budget, you will end up having more liberty to spend later on in life.

2. Live a simple life.

Proverbs 21:17 says, *"He that loveth pleasure shall be a poor man: he that loveth wine and oil shall not be rich."* God is teaching us in this verse that the person who loves to have a lot of possessions will end up being poor.

One of the mistakes of this present generation is they do not know how to live a simple life. Listen, you don't have to have everything you see. Likewise, you don't need everything you think you need. If you will learn to live a simple life, then you will never know what you are "missing out" on by not having all those "things."

When living an extravagant lifestyle, you create an appetite that you may not be able to keep up throughout your entire life. Driving a used car is not going to hurt you. Not having the latest technological device will not put you back into the Dark Ages. The food at the economical restaurant is just as good as the food at the expensive restaurant. Just because something is not a name brand does not make it a bad item. What I am saying is, you need to learn to live a more simple life. This will help you to keep your finances straight.

3. Pay your tithe.

One of the quickest ways to get your finances in a mess is to stop paying your tithe. Malachi 3:8-9 says, *"Will a man rob God? Yet ye have robbed me. But ye say, Wherein have we robbed thee? In tithes and offerings. Ye are cursed with a curse: for ye have robbed me, even this whole nation."* Notice that God says He places a curse on those who don't pay their tithe.

When a married couple gets out of the habit of paying their tithe, they will find their finances become cursed. Let me explain! You will find that the purchases you make won't last as long as they would if you had paid your tithe. When you don't pay your tithe, you will find that added expenses will come that you did not plan on. When you don't pay your tithe, you will find that your money won't go as far is it should.

There are some who read this and think they can't afford to pay their tithe. Let me make this very clear, the first thing you pay in your budget is your tithe. You can always afford to pay your tithe. Though it may not make sense to give God ten percent of your income, you will find that if you will follow God's command of tithing, He will bless your finances in a greater way. Money will tend to go further than what you thought it would. You will find your finances are in better condition, all because you pay your tithe. God blesses those who pay their tithes. Don't bring a curse upon your finances by not paying your tithe. Pay your tithes and let God bless your finances.

4. Know your balances.

Proverbs 27:23 says, *"Be thou diligent to know the state of thy flocks, and look well to thy herds."* Notice that God commands us to be diligent about knowing the *"state"* of our flocks and herds. God is commanding us to know where we stand financially.

Both husband and wife need to know how much money is in the checkbook. I am one who believes that there should be no secrets when it comes to the finances. It is wise for each spouse to know what the conditions of their finances are. When you know what your checkbook balances are, then you will be more careful about spending money.

If only one spouse knows the balance in their checkbook, then only one spouse will be more careful about spending money. When you get around spenders, many times they have no clue the amount of money they really have. This can cause strife in the marriage because the one who knows the balance will get on the one who is freely spending. Keeping a close eye on your balance will curb your appetite to spend. When you know you are getting low, it is amazing how you can cut back, all because you know your checkbook balance. Be sure to regularly keep an eye on the balance in your checkbook.

5. Let the best person run the finances.

When it comes to the finances, whoever is the best person to keep the finances straight should be the person who runs and controls the checkbook. I am not one who believes that only the husband should handle the checkbook. My reason is because there are many men who have poor spending and financial habits. If the wife is better with finances, then she should handle the checkbook and finances.

Let me give you some help in how to determine who should handle the finances. The person who handles the finances must be one who is tight with their money. The person who handles the finances should be the one who knows the value of keeping money set aside for rainy days. The person who handles the finances needs to be a person who is good with balancing a checkbook. The person who handles the finances needs to be a person who is prone to regularly watch the checkbook and spending habits. The person who handles the finances needs to be one who is capable of letting a budget tell them what to spend. This will help you in deciding who should handle the finances. Then whomever you decide to handle the finances, the other spouse needs to listen to them when it comes to their purchasing and the amount that can be spent.

6. Talk to each other before making major purchases.

Major purchases should never be made by yourself. Major purchases need to be decided upon with much caution. Proverbs 11:14 says, *"Where no counsel is, the people fall: but in the multitude of counsellors there is safety."* Counseling will help you to keep your finances in proper working order.

Though I believe that it is always wise to get outside counsel before you make a major purchase, one of the best ways to get counsel is to get each other's advice. Before you go out and borrow or spend on a major purchase, you would be wise to talk to each other about whether or not you really need that item. Sometimes one spouse will know more about the product than the other, which will help you in deciding whether or not this is a good purchase. Sometimes one spouse will pour cold water on the emotion that another has about the product.

You should both agree on major purchases together so that you go into the decision together. If one goes into a purchase alone, if that purchase ends up being a bad purchase, then that can create an area or source of strife. If one spouse does not want to make the purchase, then table it for awhile. You will find that you either didn't need it, or the other spouse will eventually come around. Don't be so selfish that you decide alone to make a major purchase.

7. Don't nickel and dime your finances to death.

Proverbs 23:5 says, *"Wilt thou set thine eyes upon that which is not? for riches certainly make themselves wings; they fly away as an eagle toward heaven."* God is teaching us in this verse that money can be spent as fast, if not faster, than you can earn it. The phrase, "Hard come, easy go" is not a cliché. Hard earned money can be spent in a heartbeat if you regularly spend money on little things.

If your budget does not allow you to purchase a certain small item, then don't purchase it. A little cup of coffee here and there can add up. The extra item you buy from the checkout line can add up real quick. If you keep track of how much those little purchases add up to, you will be amazed.

There are some who literally nickel and dime their finances to death. If you constantly make "little" purchases that don't seem to be that expensive, then you will find yourself without money in the long run.

8. Lay your credit card down.

I know that we live in a society where it seems that you can't make it without a credit card. Trust me, I know this is true. When you travel as much as I do, you quickly find out that you just about can't make it without a credit card. The problem with this is the credit card has led to the huge debt that many couples face. It is very easy to slap a credit card down without thinking, not realizing you really don't have the wherewithal to pay for that purchase. Before long you are in a mountain of debt, and you have added a mountain of stress to your marriage as well.

Using your debit card is always better than using a credit card. As long as you know the balance in your checkbook (as we discussed earlier), you will be much more careful about your spending with plastic. If at all possible, leave your credit cards at home and only use them when necessary. Some companies make you use your card periodically to keep it active, so use it occasionally, but pay the balance off at the end of the month.

9. Don't go out on a limb when borrowing money.

Proverbs 22:7 says, *"The rich ruleth over the poor, and the borrower is servant to the lender."* God warns us that when you borrow money, you become a servant to the bank that loaned the money to you. God was not saying it is wrong to borrow money, He was simply warning us about going out on a limb to borrow money.

My good friend, Dr. Russell Anderson, who God has allowed to make millions of dollars in his lifetime, says quite often when it comes to borrowing, "Climb up the tree and stay close to the tree trunk, but don't go out on the limbs. You don't know how strong they are, and when you get out there they might break." This is so true! A good rule of thumb when it comes to borrowing is to only borrow what you could pay if there was a set back in your finances. Don't borrow on your current income, borrow on an income that is lower than what you make right now.

10. Set aside for a rainy day.

This is where many couples get themselves in trouble. They spend every penny they have and live from one paycheck to the next. This is a very poor habit to get into. You will find that financial rainy days will come, but if you have money set aside, you will be able to make it through those times.

My wife and I have practiced this principle since we were first married. Because of my line of work as an evangelist, the holiday seasons are always financially a bit tighter than other times during the year because my meetings slow up. Time and again our rainy day fund has gotten us through those times. When your financial rainy days come, if you have money set aside, you will be able to make it through those times.

11. Save some purchases for later on in life.

One common mistake young couples make when they first get married is thinking they immediately need everything their parents have. What they forget is that their parents spent years acquiring their possessions. Thus, the young couple goes out and immediately gets everything, and by doing so, they get themselves into debt that they might not be able to get themselves out of for quite some time.

There are some items you need to save for and purchase later on in your marriage. This will allow you to have something to look forward to together. Get a timeline on some purchases and decide to wait before you go out and spend. Some of these items may be a new car, a vacation to an exotic destination, a larger home, etc. Start out slow and save some things for later on in life.

12. Don't window shop.

This is one of my pet peeves. I know you are saying that I am a man and that I hate shopping. Well you are partly right on that, but I have learned that if you don't go window shopping you most likely won't spend money that you don't have.

I often say, "Why go look at something that you know you can't afford to purchase." When you go window shopping, you create an appetite and you will think you must have it right now. The reason the stores put their displays out is to draw you to come into the store and make a purchase. You should only go shopping when you know what you are going to buy, and when your budget says that you can buy.

13. Stop trying to impress your peers.

The "Keeping up with the Jones'" mentality will get you into a big financial mess. Purchasing to impress everyone with how well you are doing financially will one day get you in financial trouble.

Purchasing to impress your friends will cause you to purchase a car that you really don't need. Let's face it, the clothing, cars and homes we purchase are more for status than they are for needs. When you look at your spending habits, most of what you purchase is to show others how well you are doing. If you are going to keep your finances in proper condition, then stop purchasing to impress everyone else, and purchase to meet your needs.

14. Learn to stretch your dollar.

If you will learn to stretch your dollar, you will find that you can save yourself some money in the long run. My wife is very good in this area. One of the things I appreciate about my wife is her ability to stretch the money we have so it can go as far as possible.

Here are some things you can do to stretch your dollars. Put off purchases as long as you can. This may help you to save a little extra money. Wait for the sales before purchasing something. You can save yourself a lot of money if you will wait to purchase something on sale. You should also learn to shop ahead. Waiting till the last minute to purchase something will always cause you to spend more money. Shop ahead and you will be able to find the sales. Whenever you purchase something, always ask if there is a special or discount. You might be surprised what discounts you can get by asking. Share your meals when going out to eat. Most restaurant portions are pretty large; sharing with your children or each other can save you some money. Be sure to shop around when making purchases. Don't buy from the first store you walk into. Comparison shop on the internet and at several stores before making a purchase. This way you can make sure you are getting the best deal. Finding ways to stretch your dollar will allow you to have more money in the long run.

15. Don't wait to get financial help.

It is always much easier to help someone who comes to you at the beginning of a financial struggle than it is when they are buried in debt. The earlier you get help with your finances, the quicker you will get over your financial problems. Don't let embarrassment be the thing that stops you from getting financial help.

16. Pay your bills on time.

Late fees add up very quickly. If you make it a habit to pay your bills late, you will end up spending more money than you should. Though this is common knowledge, there are many who end up repeatedly paying late fees. Late fees could be the make or break thing that decides whether or not you get ahead financially. Make it a habit to avoid paying late fees by paying your bills on time.

By keeping your finances in good shape, you take away one more thing that the Devil can use to destroy your marriage. Do your best to be financially healthy. It will take work, but the effort and results are very rewarding.

"You should always let your spouse have the right to warn you about someone who could be making advances towards you."

Chapter 11

The Strange Woman

One of the vows you said when you got married was that you would keep yourself from all others. This vow is not to be taken lightly. With the atmosphere in today's world, you will have to purposely keep your vows as society continuously attacks the monogamous relationship. Hollywood has made it seem normal to have an extra-marital affair. They have pictured it as normal for every spouse to be unfaithful. Despite what Hollywood and society would like to push, being faithful to your spouse is the right and scriptural thing to do.

Though most people feel pretty safe in their relationship with their spouse, nobody should ever feel that their marriage is beyond an extra-marital affair. Anybody in a weak moment can fall into this horrible sin, only to regret its consequences later on in life. We must constantly watch our relationships with the opposite gender so that we don't fall prey to Satan's attack against our marriages.

The Book of Proverbs carries several warnings to the married person about the strange woman. Proverbs 23:26-27 says, *"My son, give me thine heart, and let thine eyes observe my ways. For a whore is a deep ditch; and a strange woman is a narrow pit."* Notice the warning to this son was that the strange woman was like a pit, that once you fall into it, the hurt and damage is great. We are warned again in Proverbs 2:16, *"To deliver thee from the strange woman, even from the* stranger which flattereth with her words;" You can find warnings like this in Proverbs 5:3, 20; 6:24; 7:5; 20:16; and 27:13. Each time the warning to this young man was to watch out for the strange woman who would ruin his marriage.

The word *"strange"* is the same word we use for someone who is a foreigner. In other words, God was telling the man that any woman who is not his wife is a strange woman. It can also be said to the wife that any man who is not her husband is a strange man. God warns that the stranger is anyone to whom you are not married.

The word *"strange"* can be taken wrong if we don't look at this word in context. God is not talking about a whore when he talks about the strange woman. God addresses the whore and her lifestyle, but the strange woman is different from the whore. The difference is that a whore is someone you don't know, whereas the strange woman is someone you do know. In the proper context, a strange woman is any person of the opposite gender who is not your spouse. In other words, when God warns us of the strange woman, He is warning us to watch out for those with whom we work and fellowship.

If we are going to avoid the strange woman, then we need to look at her characteristics in order to avoid her. According to the Scriptures, her main characteristic is her speech. Over and over again God talks about the flattery of the strange woman. This could be the person who is constantly complimenting you and telling you how good you are. The strange woman is a smooth talker. She talks in such a way that she makes us feel good about ourselves. God says to watch out for the person who is like this.

Another characteristic of the strange woman is her attire. She dresses for people to notice her body. In other words, she dresses improperly. The strange woman is deceptive with her words. She is often times very loud when she speaks. According to the Scriptures she can be very stubborn about her advancing ways. The strange woman is one who would rather be away from her home than at home. She is a busybody. If she is married, she will degrade the values of her husband, but praise your values. Then in Proverbs 6:26, she has unchaste tendencies. In all actuality, this verse says she has the same tendencies as the whore. God is saying that the strange woman will be very flirty with men. Not quite throwing herself at them, but will be very forward in a sensual way. God warns us about these characteristics so that we don't fall for her traps. Each of these tendencies can be for the man as well as for the woman. Whether you are a husband or wife, you must watch for those who have these tendencies and could ruin your marriage.

Now that we know the characteristics of what to look for in the strange woman, over the next few pages let me give you many guidelines to help you avoid having an extra-marital affair. Let me remind you that an affair could hurt your marriage beyond repair. Staying faithful always pays good dividends. Don't listen to the lies of Satan and your flesh, for those lies may give you immediate satisfaction, but they will leave you regretting your actions for many years.

1. Don't give your spouse a reason to look around.

Though there is never a good reason for your spouse to look around, you should make sure that the needs of your spouse are met at home. God says in Proverbs 5:18-19, *"Let thy fountain be blessed: and rejoice with the wife of thy youth. Let her be as the loving hind and pleasant roe; let her breasts satisfy thee at all times; and be thou ravished always with her love."* God was teaching that the person you should be carried away with is your spouse.

Many relationships are ruined because the one spouse is not meeting the physical or emotional needs of the other spouse. You should never let another person be more loving with their words to your spouse than you are. You should always make sure that the physical needs of your spouse are met whether or not you feel like doing so. If you are not doing your part in meeting the needs of your spouse, then you could likely drive them from you to someone else. Though it is not right for them to look for their needs to be met by someone else, you don't want to one day look back and realize you could have avoided this affair by meeting the physical and emotional needs of your spouse.

2. The actions of your spouse never give you a right to do wrong.

In the Scriptures, God always holds you accountable for your own sin. Though God may judge the other person for what they have done, you are ultimately responsible for your own actions. Blaming your actions on your spouse is not acceptable to God.

Romans 14:12 says, *"So then every one of us shall give account of himself to God."* Notice that God holds you responsible for your actions. Whether or not your spouse does right is not an excuse for you to do wrong. Likewise, because they do wrong is no excuse for you to do wrong. You are to do right even if they are doing wrong. God will hold you accountable for your own actions.

3. Listen to the warnings of your spouse.

One thing my wife and I have always done in our marriage is give each other the freedom to warn the other of someone else's advances. You see, I know my wife knows women better than I do because she is a woman. She knows when a woman is flirting with me, and I want her to caution me when a woman is flirting with me. Sometimes I will think a lady is just being kind, when my wife knows that the woman is flirting with me. I've learned that my wife is right, so I listen to her.

You should always let your spouse have the right to warn you about someone who could be making advances towards you. You may say, "Bro. Domelle, my spouse is very

116

jealous." Well, you ought to be thankful that they are very jealous over you. If your spouse were not jealous, then you would have a reason to be concerned. When your spouse comes to you and warns you about someone's advance towards you, listen to them and follow their advice. Even if they are wrong, you are giving your spouse the security that you are not looking elsewhere and that you want to stay faithful to them.

4. Never be alone with the opposite gender.

This is one of those areas in today's society that seems to be forsaken. If you are married, you have no right to ever be alone with someone of the opposite gender. I don't care if it is a work related function, **YOU SHOULD NEVER BE ALONE WITH THE OPPOSITE GENDER!!!**

Very few people can be alone with the opposite gender several times without wrong thoughts beginning to enter into their minds. Pastors should be careful about counseling women alone. My opinion is, if you can't help them in a few visits, then send them to your wife. I believe it is wise to have a window in the office where you counsel so that others can see in while you are counseling a woman. In any case, guard yourself from being alone with the opposite gender. If you find yourself in a room alone, quickly get yourself out of that room where everybody can see you.

In the years that I have been in the ministry, I have seen many affairs innocently started when a man and woman spend time alone. Satan knows our weaknesses, and he will use that alone time to break down the walls that we held up with the opposite gender. He knows that when we are constantly alone with the opposite gender we will become more casual in our conversation and actions, which can ultimately lead you to be unfaithful to your spouse.

5. Don't touch the opposite gender.

Here is an area that many people need to guard against. We live in a day when we think hugging each other at church is fine. Let me be clear on this, I don't know when it is ever right for you to touch the opposite gender other than a brief shaking of the hands when greeting each other.

God says in 1 Corinthians 7:1, *"Now concerning the things whereof ye wrote unto me: It is good for a man not to touch a woman."* God knew that it is never good for a man and a woman to touch. Touching each other can lead to wrong feelings that cannot be justly met. You should always feel uncomfortable when someone from the opposite gender is constantly trying to touch you. Be careful and watch out for this person.

6. Don't become too casual with the opposite gender.

With the workplace being filled with men and women, casualness has crept into our relationships with the opposite gender. We have to remember that before a person is a casualty, they are casual.

One of the dangers you will constantly have to guard against is that of becoming casual with the opposite gender. Even with people whom you call your good friends, you must guard against the temptation of becoming casual. In the church offices, the pastoral staff must guard against becoming too casual with the church secretaries. In the workplace, if you work with the opposite gender, keep your relationship with them on a professional level and nothing more. Any email correspondence should be strictly related to work. Never allow yourself to have any communication through the phone, email or letters on a casual basis with the opposite gender. Your spouse should have total freedom to listen in on or read any correspondence at any time they choose.

7. Stay madly in love with your spouse.

I know this may seem obvious, but most people don't work on their marital relationship as they should. Never take for granted that your marriage is always going to be great. Treat your marriage as if you are trying to win your spouse over on the first date. If you don't work on keeping a fervent love for your spouse, then you will find that you will have a better chance of ruining your marriage through an extra-marital affair.

8. Realize that the other person has weaknesses as well.

One of the biggest lies people swallow when having an affair is that the person they are involved with doesn't have any problems. We must realize that everybody has flaws in their life. Just because we have been hit with a stupid stick and are blinded by our lust does not mean that the person you want to involve yourself with is the perfect person. If they were that great, then they would not be interested in ruining your relationship.

Think about this, if they are willing to cause you to run around on your spouse, then what will stop them from doing the same thing somewhere else down the road to you? The only reason why you think the other person is better than your spouse is because you have allowed selfishness and sin to blind you. Whenever a person leaves their spouse for someone else, they are going from one problem to a bigger problem. Stay with your spouse and work out your problems. That is always the best solution to the problem.

9. Don't watch the wrong things.

One of the biggest contributors to extra-marital affairs is what people watch. You will have a hard time staying faithful to your spouse when you watch movies that show people running around on their spouse.

119

Many times what we call love stories should be called lust stories. Hollywood rarely produces anything that is not filled with lust. If you want to keep your relationship with your spouse right, then stay away from their productions.

Likewise, be careful with what you look at on the internet and in magazines. Everything you look at on the internet should be viewable to your spouse. If your spouse would not want you looking at a certain website, then you have no business looking at it. Filling your mind with the filth of pornographic websites will fill your mind with thoughts that will destroy your marriage. Stay away from anything that would pollute your mind and ruin your marriage.

Let me put it this way, don't create an appetite that you cannot scripturally fulfill. When you look at wrong pictures, you create an appetite of which you know God does not approve. The only thing the appetite of wrong pictures will promote is your taking it to the next level. Avoid it like the plague and never look at wrong pictures.

10. Don't do something you will regret later on in life.

Every action in life has consequences. Before you ruin your marriage, you better decide if you are willing to live with the consequences. Are you willing to live with child support for years down the road? Are you willing to live with your children having a split home relationship? Are you willing to cause your children to lose every bit of respect they had for you because you were unfaithful to your spouse? You better consider these thoughts, for this is what you will have to live with if you ever start a relationship with someone other than your spouse.

11. Don't destroy what you have worked so hard to build.

Many times I have watched someone ruin their life's work for an extra-marital affair. All the years of sacrifice will be ruined with a one-night stand. All the years of building a ministry can be ruined with an affair. Being unfaithful to your spouse can ruin all the sweat, blood and tears you've invested in your marriage.

If you would consider what you are about ready to give up all for the sake of physical pleasure, then I believe you would never partake of this wicked act. Listen, you've worked so hard to get where you are, don't blow it for a relationship with some other person.

12. Think about the hurt you will bring to your children.

The ones who always suffer the most in an affair are the children. Yes, the other spouse may eventually get over the hurt and move on, but the children live with the results of the affair for the rest of their lives.

Don't break the hearts of your children by being selfish. Stop thinking about yourself and start thinking about the ones whom you love. Look at the face of your children and ask yourself how you are going to explain your actions to them. You will hurt your children more than you will ever know. Don't do something that will cause them to lose the respect that they now have for you.

13. Dress properly at all times.

One of the things that starts this whole process off is the way people dress. With the scantily clothed women and the men running around like they are playing on a beach somewhere, it's no wonder that people are unfaithful to their spouses.

Your clothing says a lot about your character. I have said for years, "If you're not for sale, then don't advertise yourself." In other words, stop showing off your body so that the opposite gender will lust after it. Being properly dressed will cause a mystique about you that will keep the wrong type of person away from you. Furthermore, being properly dressed will cause you to act properly. The more casual you dress, the more you become casual with other people. Dress right, if for no other reason than to keep your relationship with others proper.

14. Stay away from social networking sites.

One of most dangerous things going on in the home today is the social networking websites. People will say things on these sites that they would never say to someone face to face. Let me make this as clear as I can, nobody has any business having a social network account. If you want to talk to people, then call them. Who better to talk to about what is on your heart other than your spouse? My advice to you is to cancel any accounts you may have or never join any of these sites. At the best they are unhealthy for your social skills, and at the worst you will get involved with someone who can ruin your marriage. Stay away!!!

15. Get help when you are having problems.

When you are having marital problems, immediately get help. When you are having problems with adulterous thoughts, then immediately go get some help. It is better to get help early than to do something you'll regret later when you're trying to put the pieces of your life back together. As soon as you see a problem in your marriage, immediately get help.

16. Always sign notes to the opposite gender from you and your spouse.

One practice that my wife and I have done for years is when a personal note is written to the opposite gender, we always address it from the both of us. If I write something to a lady, it will either be done on my business letterhead or signed by my wife and me. If you sign just your name then that person could take it the wrong way, which could eventually lead to a problem.

17. Ask God to keep you from the temptation of adultery.

Who better to help you to stay away from anything that would lead to adultery than God? You should daily ask God to lead you away from those moments of temptation. If you can stay away from temptation, then you will be able to stay away from the sin itself. Though you might think that this is admitting you have a problem, in all reality you are simply admitting that you are human and that you don't ever want to be faced with that moment when you must make your stand.

Christian, the strange woman will destroy your life. Anyone who has ever yielded to her invitation has always regretted that moment later in life. Make it a point in your marriage to never allow that time of indiscretion to come. Protect your marriage by keeping it healthy and by constantly avoiding the strange woman.

"Mind reading is not part of the vows of marriage."

Chapter 12

Communication

Communication is one of the most important ingredients in having a winning team. Poor communication between players and coaches will cause poor performance on the field. Poor communication between the players in a game will give the other team an advantage, and can also cause a loss. Communication is very important in order to have a winning team.

When playing sports, if you don't know what your teammate is doing, then that will cause confusion on the field. Confusion on the field will cause frustration in the huddle. Eventually frustration will lead to fighting between players. When you get players fighting with each other, then you will lose the game because you are focusing your energy on the wrong thing. Fighting players should be focusing their energy on the opposing team and not on their disagreements with teammates. All of this happens because of poor communication between players.

I have said many times that a marriage should consist of a husband and wife working together like a team. When a husband and wife become teammates in life, it is amazing what they can do together. One thing that will destroy the teamwork of a husband and wife is poor communication. It is very important that you learn to properly communicate with your spouse.

Your goal in your marriage should be to win. Winning in marriage is having a happy marriage and working together till death. Just staying together does not mean that you have a winning marriage. I have seen people who will not get divorced, but are losing in their marriage because of their poor communication. Don't get me wrong, I am thrilled that they have chosen to stay together, but their marriage could be much better if they would learn to communicate with each other. If you want your marriage to be a winning marriage, then you and your spouse need to learn how to properly communicate with each other.

The Scriptures say in Ephesians 5:28-29, *"So ought men to love their wives as their own bodies. He that loveth his wife loveth himself. For no man ever yet hated his own flesh; but nourisheth and cherisheth it, even as the Lord the church:"* Notice in this verse that God talks about the husband nourishing his marriage. The word "nourish" means, "to feed." In other words, God is commanding the husband to feed his marriage so that he can help make his marriage successful.

I have found that one of the best ways to feed your marriage is through communication. Throughout the Scriptures God speaks of the importance of communicating properly. For instance, in 1 Timothy 6:18, God says that we should be *"...willing to communicate."* God commands the wife to be careful about her conversation to her husband in 1 Peter 3:1-2 when He says, *"Likewise, ye wives, be in subjection to your own husbands; that, if any obey not the word, they also may without the word be won by the conversation of the wives; While they behold your chaste conversation coupled with fear."* So not only did God command the husband to communicate with the wife, but He also commanded the wife to communicate with her husband.

Communication is very important for a happy marriage. Without proper communication, a husband and wife will never enjoy marriage as God intended. Your marriage will suffer if you don't learn to properly communicate with your spouse.

You should want your spouse to be the one whom you can communicate with easier than anyone else. Let me give you several thoughts that will help you to better communicate with your spouse.

1. It takes two to communicate.

Communication is never one-sided. You are not communicating when one side is doing all of the talking. In order to have communication, both parties must be involved. For instance, when you contact someone and they respond back to you, then you can say that you have established communication with them.

You need to do your best to establish communication with your spouse. One side doing all the talking is not communication. Too many marriages today have one-sided communication. Then they wonder why they are having marriage problems. Both you and your spouse must understand that both of you must be involved in a conversation in order to truly have communication.

2. Both sides must be willing to talk in order to communicate.

One of the biggest mistakes that you can make is to assume that your spouse knows what you want or what you are frustrated about. Let me be blunt with you; your spouse is not a mind reader. You must never take for granted that your spouse knows what you are thinking. Mind reading is not part of the vows of marriage. If you were to look with an open mind at many of the problems you have faced in your marriage, you would see there is a lack of communication. As if your spouse was a mind reader, you assumed they should know what you're thinking. The problem is your spouse is not a mind reader, therefore you must learn not to assume that they know what you are thinking.

127

If you are going to solve problems in your marriage, or if you are going to accomplish a task together, then both sides must learn to talk. Not scream and yell, talk! Yelling and screaming are not communicating. Talking reasonably with each other is communicating. Though your personality may be one that you don't talk much, you must learn to open up to your spouse and talk with them if you are going to establish communication in your marriage.

3. Both husband and wife must learn to listen in order to have proper communication.

Part of communicating is listening. If both sides are talking and neither is listening, then you are not communicating with each other. I fear too many times this is one of the biggest culprits of the lack of communication in a marriage. Because both sides are passionate about their point being understood, they fail to listen to their spouse and only want to tell their side. If you want your spouse to listen to you, then you need to learn to listen to them. This is communication.

Listening is not having a glazed look over your face as your spouse is talking to you. Just like you don't like it when your children zone you out when you are talking to them, your spouse doesn't like it either when you zone them out. When you and your spouse are having a conversation, listen. Stop thinking about everything else and listen. Stop listening to the noise of their voice, and listen to the words they are saying. If you would learn to listen, you might find there is something you can do to help solve some problems in your marriage. Though you are not talking when they are talking, zoning out your spouse as they talk is not considered listening. Control your mind and pay attention to what your spouse is saying.

Furthermore, listening is something that both husband and wife should do. It is not communication if one side is doing all the talking. Communication is one side talking while the other side is listening, and then reversing roles in the talking and listening part. If you are going to have good communication skills with your spouse, then the best way to do this is to allow both sides to have a part in the talking and the listening. Let your spouse talk for awhile and then you talk. Don't have a one-sided conversation. Both sides must be involved in the talking and in the listening.

4. Communication takes time.

You will never have good communication with your spouse without taking time to talk to each other. Just because you say a few words to each other every day does not qualify you as having good communication in your marriage. In order to have clear communication, it takes time to iron out any misunderstandings that you or your spouse may have.

Because it takes time to have good communication with your spouse, you will have to learn to purposely set aside some time every week, and in some cases every day, in order to communicate. I have found that it works well for my wife and I to go out and eat at a restaurant so we can have some time to communicate with each other. It may be that you and your spouse go for a drive in the car and talk to each other then. Whatever you do, be sure you are alone during these times. Talking to your spouse in front of your friends is not a good time for quality communication. Communication must be done privately in order for both sides to understand each other clearly.

Likewise, your children don't need to know all of the business or problems that you and your spouse need to talk about. There are times when your communication may be about intimacy with each other, and this is not your children's business. Likewise, sometimes you may need to communicate with each other on how you are going to handle the finances. Again, your children don't need to know if you are struggling financially. If you are going to have good communication with your spouse, you will need to learn to have some time alone without the children being around. There are some things that only you and your spouse need to know. Your marriage is between you and your spouse, not you and your children. Yes, your children are a part of the family, but we are working on the marriage, and proper communication cannot be established with the children present. Learn to talk to each other alone.

5. Communication takes honesty.

Honesty is very important in order to have proper communication. God commands us in Ephesians 4:25, *"Wherefore putting away lying, speak every man truth with his neighbour: for we are members one of another."* This command to speak truth with your neighbor is also talking about your spouse. Not only should you be truthful with those outside of your marriage and family, but most importantly you should be truthful with your spouse.

If your spouse finds out that you are not being honest in your conversation, then you will hurt the lines of communication. Dishonesty will cause a person not to trust you quicker than anything else. You must learn to be honest with your spouse when you are talking to each other in order to solve any problems that you may have. When being truthful, be tactful as well. Don't be so blunt with truth that you blow your spouse out of the water. Honesty is an important ingredient in good communication.

6. Communication is never established without respect for your spouse.

You should never be rude to your spouse when you are communicating with them. Though you may be addressing a touchy subject, disrespecting your spouse is never acceptable. For instance, calling your spouse a "jerk" should **NEVER** be an option. Calling names or cursing your spouse is disrespectful and you will never accomplish anything with this kind of talk. When addressing serious problems with your spouse, you must **ALWAYS** leave your spouse with their dignity. Being rude and cursing your spouse is the quickest way to get into a shouting match, and that is certainly not communication.

Remember this is your spouse to whom you are talking. Don't talk to your spouse as if they are a child; talk to them like they are your spouse. Communication is not informing them what you want done; communication is talking respectfully to your spouse giving them ample time to explain their mind in a respectful way.

7. Communication needs clear understanding to work.

In order for communication to be successful in your marriage, you must have a clear understanding of what your spouse is trying to say. When you are discussing something with your spouse, you need to be sure that you both leave the conversation with a clear understanding of what the other spouse wants or sees.

If you don't understand what your spouse is trying to get across to you, then politely ask them to explain what they mean. Leaving a conversation without an understanding of what was discussed will only cause frustration later on when one side thought they had already discussed something.

As we previously discussed, be honest with your spouse when you are talking. Don't expect them to automatically understand what you are talking about just because you understand. If you want your spouse to do something, then don't assume they know what you want them to do, but tell them exactly what you want them to do. Your subtle hints to your spouse of what you want done do not give a clear understanding. As obvious as you may think your hints are, sometimes your spouse just won't see it. To avoid frustration on both sides, be very clear about what you want your spouse to do.

8. Communicate in or with proper tones.

Sometimes we can come across more abruptly than what we realize. I believe we are all guilty of this. The tone in how you converse with your spouse is just as important as what you say to your spouse. When you talk with your spouse, be careful how you come across. Listen to yourself as you talk. Don't be so flippant in what you say, for your speech can come across as careless, or sometimes abrupt, and at other times as if you are upset.

As we have previously discussed in this chapter, yelling at each other is never proper. When you get into a shouting match with your spouse, you will only end the conversation with harm being done to your relationship. Always avoid raising your voice to your spouse. Remember, they are the love of your life; treat them like you love them and not like you would treat your enemy. Sometimes we treat the ones we love the most the worst. Don't be guilty of this. Not only should you watch what you say, but also watch how you say something. Listen to yourself as you talk, and if you come across wrong, then apologize.

9. At times good communication takes restraint.

You don't always need to say what is on your mind. This mentality that you need to unload what you are thinking can cause serious harm to your marital relationship. In order to keep the communication proper in your marriage, at times you will have to practice restraint. Remember that you don't always have to give a piece of your mind.

For instance, if you are highly upset at the moment, then the best action you can take at that time is to get away until you cool down. If you are upset with your spouse, sometimes silence is the best form of communication. I am not talking about the silent treatment, I am talking about you just keeping your mouth shut to avoid saying something you will regret later on. Your tongue can get you into a lot of trouble. To keep the lines of communication open, you will have to restrain yourself from saying things at certain times when what you want to say would hurt your relationship.

10. Communication takes trust.

You will never be successful in having good communication with your spouse if they can't trust you to not tell everybody what you have talked about. When your spouse has told you something in confidence, you must keep it confidential. Everything that goes on in your marriage is not everyone else's business. There are many things in marriage that need to be kept in the marriage. Trust is an important part of any marriage. When trust is violated, then you will have a hard time establishing that trust again.

What you and your spouse talk about in private should never be discussed with your family. The privacy of your marriage is not your family's business. Likewise, you should not tell everything you and your spouse talk about to your good friend. Listen, your spouse should be your best friend, so why would you want to tell anybody else what you two have discussed? When your spouse feels that you will tell others what you have privately talked about, then you will never establish the trust that is needed for good communication.

The only time you should ever talk to someone else about private marital issues is when you are going to your pastor for counsel. Even at this point, there are some things you should not talk about with your pastor. Some information is only for the husband and the wife. Your pastor can help you with your marriage, but no one else should ever hear the private conversations that take place in your marriage.

Good communication is a very important part of having a happy marriage. Work on the communication in your marriage. Good communication will allow you both to understand what it is that you are trying to accomplish together.

"*It does not matter what your spouse has done, somehow you must find it in yourself to forgive them.*"

Chapter 13

Hotel or Home

One of my favorite times every week is when I leave the hotel room to go home to be with my wife and daughter. In all my years of traveling as an evangelist, I have spent several thousands of nights in a hotel room. Trust me when I say this, I lost the thrill of staying in a hotel room a long time ago.

I would much rather be at home with my family than spend another night in a hotel. Hotels are lonely and uncomfortable. Hotels are impersonal and the walls won't talk to you. As nice as they try to make a hotel room, it just cannot replace being at home. As much as they try to make hotel rooms with a home-like atmosphere, it just can't measure up to being at home with my wife and family.

One sad thing I see today is that many marriages are like a hotel and not a home. What I mean by this is that there are couples who live in the same house, but they never spend time with each other or spend time talking to each other. Their marriage left being a home a long time ago and became a marriage that is just like a hotel.

Marriage was never intended to be a miserable institution. Some feel that they have been institutionalized in their marriage. Yet, when God instituted marriage He intended for it to be a happy institution. God did not intend for a couple to dwell together and never have time for each other. God intended for a husband and wife to love each other and be best friends. If husband and wife are best friends, then they will enjoy being with each other.

Your marriage is either a hotel or a home. Your marriage is nothing more than a hotel if you and your spouse never spend time with each other. You can be in the same house, but never spend time with each other, and this is the same as spending the night in a hotel. If your marriage is going to be a home, then you and your spouse need to spend time communicating with each other.

God said in Psalm 133:1, *"Behold, how good and how pleasant it is for brethren to dwell together in unity!"* God said that it would be a delightful thing for you and your spouse to dwell together in unity, but the only way this will be accomplished is for the both of you to learn to communicate with each other. God asks in Amos 3:3, *"Can two walk together, except they be agreed?"* God knew that the only way you and your spouse will ever be able to dwell together in unity is to walk together. When you are walking together you are communicating.

In the previous chapter, I talked about what it would take in order for the husband and wife to be able to communicate. In this chapter I want to expand on that thought and show you what robs a couple of the capability of communicating. Listen, if you and your spouse don't communicate with each other, then you have made your marriage like that lonely hotel room that I stay in when I am on the road. The Devil is out to destroy the communication lines between you and your spouse. You will have to do everything in your power not to let anything rob you of communicating so your marriage is a true home and not a hotel. Let me show you several things that rob your marriage of proper communication.

1. Sin

God says in Psalm 66:18, *"If I regard iniquity in my heart, the Lord will not hear me:"* Always remember, your relationship with your spouse is a picture of your relationship with God. So, if sin would block you from talking to God, then sin will block your communication with your spouse.

When you are hiding sin in your life, you are going to be guarded when you talk to your spouse. Sin always robs a person of their joy because it keeps them from being able to open up to the ones whom they love. You will never be able to have a good marriage relationship with your spouse until you clean your life of sin. Sin will cause you to constantly guard your life, and this will cause you to become reclusive in your communication with your spouse. Don't allow sin to be the culprit that robs your marriage of proper communication. Clean up your life so that you and your spouse can have proper communication.

2. Bitterness

One of the most ignored areas that will rob you of proper communication is the sin of bitterness. God tells us in Ephesians 4:31, *"Let all bitterness...be put away from you..."* God knew that bitterness over something that happened to you in the past would hurt your marriage. Not dealing with bitterness will hurt the ability of you and your spouse to be able to properly communicate with each other.

There are many people who have allowed bad circumstances in their past to hinder their relationship with their spouse. Whether or not you realize it, until you deal with bitterness over past situations, you will hurt your ability to be able to communicate with your spouse. What you may not realize is when you hold bitterness against someone, that bitterness can come up when you are trying to communicate with your spouse and may cause you to get angry with the one you love. There are certain topics that you and your spouse cannot talk about because of bitterness. There are certain things you cannot enjoy in your marriage because of bitterness. Bitterness will eventually cause you to have a bitter marriage because it will hurt your ability to properly communicate with your spouse.

If there is something bad that has happened to you in the past that you are still bitter about today, then you better get some help from your pastor so you don't hurt your relationship with your spouse. Bitterness is a communication robber. Don't let your bitterness against someone else ruin your relationship with the one whom you love.

3. Unsettled differences

Not settling a difference that you and your spouse have had in the past will eventually rob you of proper communication. God says in Ephesians 4:26, *"Be ye angry, and sin not: let not the sun go down upon your wrath:"* Notice that God commands us to settle differences with each other before the sun goes down. The reason why is because God knows that if we don't settle them right away they will eventually hurt our communication and relationship with our spouse.

When you and your spouse have a disagreement, you better get that settled before you leave each other or before you go to bed. You should never go to bed with unsettled differences with each other. If you have to stay up all night to get those differences settled in a Christian way, then you need to stay up all night and settle them. Likewise, you should never leave each other's presence with unsettled differences. You should never walk out of the house slamming the door and driving off in anger. Settle your differences before you leave each other's presence.

There are two reasons why you should settle your differences before you go to bed or before you leave each other's presence. The first reason is because you don't want your last time with them to be a time when you were arguing. Can you imagine how bad you would feel for the rest of your life if your spouse died at night or in a car accident right after you had an unsettled difference with each other? You don't want that hanging over your head for the rest of your life. Secondly, if you don't settle your differences like the Scriptures tell you to, then you will end up hurting your communication with your spouse. Unsettled differences with your spouse will fester and hurt your ability to have proper communication. Until you get those differences settled, that grudge will be held inside and can eventually turn into bitterness. Settle all differences properly and immediately so you don't allow them to rob you of proper communication with your spouse.

4. Uncontrolled anger

God reminds us again in Ephesians 4:31 to *"Let all bitterness, and wrath… be put away from you…"* The word *"wrath"* is talking about uncontrolled anger. This is talking about a person who blows up and becomes violent.

Let me make this very clear, there is no excuse for violence in any marriage. Whether it is the man being violent with his wife or the wife being violent with her husband; both are wrong and uncalled for. Your background does not cause you to be violent; it is your uncontrolled anger that causes you to be violent. Your ethnicity has nothing to do with you being violent with your spouse; your uncontrolled anger is the cause. Whatever your excuse is for violence in your marriage, it is a poor excuse! If you're a man who beats his wife, then you are a poor excuse of a man. If you're a woman who is violent with your husband, then you're a poor excuse for a lady. Neither man nor woman should be violent with their spouse.

The only reason why you would be violent in your marriage is because of uncontrolled anger. Uncontrolled anger will keep you and your spouse from being able to properly communicate. They will be afraid every time you have a disagreement that you will become violent or blow up if they were to honestly try to talk to you about it. If you have a problem with your anger, please get some help so it won't rob you of proper communication.

5. Poor listening habits

It is very hard to have good communication with your spouse when your listening habits are very poor. The ability to be able to sit and listen to your spouse talk without always having to give your two cents worth will take character and self-control.

The present generation in which we live has been raised on the television. The television has hurt people's ability to hold their own attention for any length of time. If you don't believe me, then let me ask you this question. How long does it take for the preacher to preach before your mind starts to wander? The reason why is because television has trained your mind to have a short attention span.

This short attention span has caused many people to have poor listening habits. If a spouse stays on the same subject for any length of time, then our minds begin to wander. You must work hard at improving your listening skills. The best way to accomplish this is to stop doing whatever it is you're doing when your spouse is talking to you, and give them your undivided attention. Poor listening habits will rob you of having proper communication with your spouse.

6. Unforgiveness

Unforgiveness in your marriage will rob you and your spouse of proper communication. Colossians 3:13 says, *"Forbearing one another, and forgiving one another, if any man have a quarrel against any: even as Christ forgave you, so also do ye."* When a couple is not willing to forgive each other for the wrongs they have done, then they will never have true communication.

It does not matter what your spouse has done, somehow you must find it in yourself to forgive them. Certainly if God can forgive us after all that we did to Him, then with His help you can learn to forgive your spouse for what they have done to you. Even as hurtful as it may have been, you must learn to forgive them. If you choose not to forgive your spouse when they do wrong, then that cloud of unforgiveness will hang over every conversation you have with each other.

Remember, forgiveness is an act of the wronged; it is not an act of the one who did the wrong. Only you have the power to forgive your spouse. They cannot make you forgive them; you must choose to forgive them. Until you forgive your spouse, you will rob your marriage of proper communication, which will rob your marriage of its joy.

7. Television

For decades the television has robbed marriages and families of proper communication. Sitting down in the living room and watching television is not communication. Communication is two people talking, and when you're watching television you are not talking, instead the television is entertaining you.

Though I am not dealing with the television itself in this book, you must realize that the television really doesn't offer your marriage or family much of anything. Most of what is on the television will only hurt the ability of the husband, wife and children to be able to communicate with each other. If you don't believe me, then see what happens when you start talking in the middle of the next television program your spouse is intensely watching. That power button on your remote is a wonderful switch to use so that you and your spouse can learn to communicate with each other. Don't let the television rob your marriage of proper communication.

8. Hobbies

Before I dive into this topic, let me say that I do believe that it is good to have a hobby. A hobby is a good way to allow yourself a release from the pressure and stress of life.

What you must be careful of is that you don't allow your hobby to rob time from your spouse. There are many husbands and wives who would love to spend time with their spouse, but can't because a hobby is keeping them from each other.

Let me explain! One of the hobbies that I enjoy is playing golf; well at least I enjoy participating in golf. I'm not sure what I do qualifies as playing golf. Because a round of golf can take quite a long time, I must be careful that I don't allow my hobby to take away time from my wife. I don't play golf as much as I would like for one main reason, I would rather spend time with my wife than I would with my golf clubs. As I stated earlier, I would much rather kiss my wife than kiss my golf clubs. Those golf clubs don't return any affection to me like my wife can. If anything, they return frustration more than satisfaction. I have learned that if I want to have proper communication with my wife, then I occasionally have to give up time with my hobby.

Though your hobby may be something you do in the home, if it takes you away from your spouse, then cut back on the amount of time you spend participating in your hobby. Don't spend all your time doing your hobby when your spouse is home and in a different room. If you're not careful, your hobby will rob you of communicating with your spouse.

9. Internet and social networking

One of the things that robs marriages today of communication is the internet and social networking. Husbands and wives spend countless numbers of hours browsing the internet when they could be spending time together. What a shame that you would allow the internet to rob time that belongs to your spouse! I know you're saying right now, "I don't spend that much time on the internet." The truth is, you really don't know how much time you spend on the internet. I dare you to get a stopwatch and time how much time you spend weekly on the internet. I believe you would see that you spend way too much time online when you could be spending time with your spouse. There are many people who are addicted to the internet, and it is robbing them of valuable time they could have with their spouse.

Likewise, social networking has robbed many marriages of good communication. Let me make this very clear, nobody has any business on the social networking sites. Though there may be some good that can be done with those sites, there is more bad that happens. You will spend time on social networking sites having private conversations with people you don't even know, when the truth is you have someone you love inside of your house to whom you could talk. Don't let social networking rob your spouse of their time with you.

10. Job

This point is only for a few people, but I include it because I know there are some who never learn how to leave their job and spend some time with their spouse. There are two areas we must be careful about when it comes to our job robbing us of time with our spouse.

First, don't work so many hours that the only time you are home is to get a bite to eat and then sleep. There are many ladies who sit at home as a widow even though their husband is still alive. Their husband works so many hours that the wife hardly gets any time with him. If this is you, then you need to understand that your job is not worth ruining your marriage. What is the value of your job if your marriage is gone? Learn to be balanced between work and home.

Sometimes you may have to say "no" to your boss because you need some time with your spouse.

Secondly, there are some who take their work home. I'm all for working, but when you come home you need to leave your work on the job. I promise you, that work will still be there tomorrow. When you come home from work, come home to be home.

Lastly concerning work, don't be one who is constantly nagging your spouse about all the time they spend at work. There is nothing wrong with your spouse working more than eight hours a day, but the purpose of what I have said is for those who are **never** home with their spouse. Your job is valuable, but not worth the expense of ruining your marriage.

11. No time alone

The last area that will rob you of communicating with your spouse is never having time alone. There are many couples who never leave their children to spend time with each other. This is wrong! One day your children will be gone. Until then you better nurture your relationship with your spouse so that when they are gone you still have a relationship. The best way I have found to take care of this is to schedule time each week to spend alone with your spouse. It may be for a few hours a week, but those few hours are important for the sake of the communication in your marriage.

You marriage is either going to be a true home or more like a hotel. If you allow things to rob you of time with your spouse, then you will end up having a hotel as your home. Yes, you and your spouse may live there together, but that will be the extent of it. If you learn to not allow things to rob you of communication time with your spouse, then you will enjoy the pleasures that God wanted you to enjoy by having a true home.

Chapter 14

Winning the Heart of Your Spouse

One of the greatest victories you will achieve in your marriage will be winning the heart of your spouse. A marriage will never be what it ought to be until both husband and wife give their hearts to each other.

The heart of a person is the most valuable thing a person can have. When you have the heart of someone, then you will be able to get them to do anything that you want them to do. The father in the book of Proverbs said to his son in Proverbs 23:26, *"My son, give me thine heart, and let thine eyes observe my ways."* The father knew that if he had the heart of his son then he would be able to guide his son to do right. Likewise if the husband or wife has the heart of their spouse, then they will be able to guide their spouse to do anything they want.

God warns us in Proverbs 4:23, *"Keep thy heart with all diligence; for out of it are the issues of life."* Whoever you give your heart to is the one who will guide the direction of your life. This is why you should not give your heart to just anyone. You should guard your heart, and be sure to only give it to those to whom God would want you to give it.

Your spouse should have the right to have your heart. Delilah said to Samson in Judges 16:15, *"And she said unto him, How canst thou say, I love thee, when thine heart is not with me? thou hast mocked me these three times, and hast not told me wherein thy great strength lieth."* You will notice that Delilah was after Samson's heart, not so she could love him, but because she wanted to destroy him.

Delilah made a very true statement when she said to Samson, *"...How canst thou say, I love thee, when thine heart is not with me?"* The truth is if you really love your spouse then you will give them your heart. The ultimate measuring stick of how much you love your spouse is do they have your heart? If your spouse does not have your heart, then you do not love them as you should and vice versa.

There is a danger in giving your heart to someone. To whomever you give your heart, you give them the greatest power to hurt you as well. Yes, giving your heart to your spouse is a risky thing because they can hurt you deeply when they have your heart. But, they cannot love you to the degree you desire to be loved until you give them your heart.

A heart is a very fragile thing. When someone gives you their heart, you should never take it for granted. When someone gives you their heart, they are entrusting you with the greatest degree of trust a human can give to another. You will only give your heart to someone you trust. Therefore, when your spouse gives you their heart, treat it carefully as if it is a very breakable object. When they give you their heart, they trust you will treat it with care. What an honor when someone gives you their heart. When your spouse gives you their heart, they have given you the greatest amount of love and trust they can ever give.

Your goal in your marriage should be to invest trust in the heart of your spouse so they will trust you with their heart. This project to gain the heart of your spouse will not happen overnight. In fact, it will take a long time to win the heart of your spouse, and it will be an ongoing work until the day you die. Let me give you some advice on winning the heart of your spouse.

1. Give your spouse a reason to give you their heart.

Just because you are married to them does not mean they should just hand their heart over to you. Please don't get me wrong, I do believe you ought to give your heart to your spouse, but this is something that is earned. This is part of the reason why we date. When you date someone, you are trying to gain enough trust for that person to give you their heart.

This journey to gain the heart of your spouse should not end on the day you get married. Though your spouse gave you a portion of their heart when they agreed to marry you, they have not given you their whole heart. They gave you as much of their heart as they could at that time, but the rest of their heart can only be given after marriage. This will happen when you have given them a reason to give you their heart. Just because you wear a ring on your finger and you carry the title of their spouse does not mean that you deserve to have their heart. You earn the heart of your spouse by the way you live and by the way you treat them. If you want your spouse to give you their heart, then give them a reason to give you their heart.

2. Learn to listen.

Though I have dealt with this in previous chapters of this book, again let me stress the importance of listening to your spouse when they talk. Part of the reason you should listen to them is so they will give you their heart.

Let me ask you, why should your spouse give you their heart if you won't listen to them when they talk? If you don't have enough courtesy to listen to them when they talk, then they will never trust you with their heart.

147

When your spouse speaks to you, stop what you are doing and listen to them. When they talk to you, look them in the eyes and listen. Don't just listen to the words they are saying, but listen to their heart as they speak. Listening is a very important ingredient in earning the trust necessary for your spouse to give you their heart. This is why often times your spouse will ask you what they just said. They want to know that you are listening to them so that they can decide if they truly want to give you their heart. Your spouse will not give you their heart until you learn to listen intently to what they say to you, especially during times when their heart has been hurt.

3. Treat your spouse like a human.

Men, your wife is not your maid. She is not there for you to boss around. She is your wife. You should treat her like a wife and not like you would treat someone you've hired. Pick up after yourself around the house. Though you may think I am being a little petty, when your wife sees that you don't think of her as your maid and that you are willing to pick up after yourself around the house, this will go a long way in winning her heart. Nowhere in the Scriptures does it say that men ought to be slobs. In fact, if you have character you will pick up after yourself.

Likewise ladies, your husband is not your child. When you start trying to boss your husband around like he is a little child, then you are ruining the opportunity for him to give you his heart. Let me make this very clear, you are not your husband's mother. I know this comes as a shock to you, but there are many ladies who boss their husbands around to the point that he will never entrust his heart to her. I have seen ladies literally embarrass their husbands in front of everyone. This is not the way to gain the heart of your husband. Treat him with respect and dignity; he is your husband.

148

4. Help your spouse with their chores.

Men, if you want to win the heart of your wife, then you would be wise to help your wife with her chores around the house. For instance, it would do you good to do the laundry every once in awhile. Likewise, you could help your wife do the dishes after supper. You say, "Why would I want to do that?" Maybe you would do this because you are trying to win the heart of your wife. When she sees that you are willing to help her with the chores around the house, this will grab her attention. If you must, grab the vacuum cleaner and sweep the house. You may have to pick her up from a cardiac arrest, but you will win some points to gain her heart.

Ladies, if you want to win the heart of your husband, then help him with his chores. You must realize that if your husband is the sole bread-winner, there are many times he is worn out and doesn't feel like doing all of his household chores. This is not to say that you are not worn out too, but it is nice when you help him do his chores. When he mows the lawn, grab the weed-eater and trim the yard. When he carries the trash out, help him carry the cans to the street. I think you get the picture of what I am trying to say. If you will help him instead of bossing him, he will want to do things to make you happy because you have given him a reason to give you his heart.

5. Pamper your spouse without ulterior motives.

Here is one of those areas that both of you will have to work on. Many times when a spouse does something special, they are wondering what you are trying to get out of them.

Men, you should do what you can to pamper your wife without the motive of physical intimacy. There are times when you should massage her back and feet without an ulterior motive. Many times a wife will think that the only time she gets pampered is when her husband wants to have his physical needs met. This ought not be! At times, you should pamper

149

your wife for no other reason than because you feel she deserves it. This will certainly help you in winning her heart.

Ladies, you shouldn't spoil your husband just so you can get him to buy something for you that you have been wanting for a long time. Many times the only time a wife spoils her husband is when she wants something from him. There are times when you should spoil your husband for no reason other than that you love him. He should not feel that the only time you try to spoil him is to get something out of him. Spoiling your husband will help you in the long run to win his heart.

6. Cancel your hobby for your spouse.

Now I am really starting to tread on thin ice. Imagine canceling your shopping trip with your friends to spend time with your husband. Now why would you want to do that? Imagine canceling your golf game to spend time with your wife. I know, you think I've gone off the deep end.

The truth is, if you are going to win the heart of your spouse then you need to prove to them, at times, that they are more important than anything else in your life including your hobbies. When your hobby is more important that spending time with your spouse, why should they ever give you their heart? The heart of your spouse will be held in reserve until they see that you are willing to cancel anything for them.

Listen, life is not all about you and what you get. When you got married, you chose to give your life and heart to your spouse. That means even giving up some of the things you enjoy doing just to be with them. I promise you, having the heart of your spouse is much more fulfilling than enjoying your hobby.

7. Do your best to let your spouse have their way.

Marriage is not all about you! In fact, if you want your marriage to be happy then you will make your marriage all about your spouse. Now I know this goes against the modern philosophy that you should get what's coming to you, but you will have a hard time winning the heart of your spouse if you don't live for them.

I have learned that one of the ways to gain the heart of your spouse is to let them have their way as much as possible. For instance, if your spouse wants to go to a restaurant and you don't, then give up your will so they can enjoy the restaurant of their choice. One way my wife and I do this is we take turns choosing which restaurant to go to. When it's my turn to pick which restaurant we are going to eat at, I give her two restaurants I would like to go to and then she picks the one she prefers. When it's her turn to pick, then she does the same. This is how we have learned to let each other have their way.

Letting your spouse have their way will help you to win their heart. When they see you are not out to hurt them, but to please them, they will be more willing to hand over their heart to you.

8. Listen for their desires and try to fulfill them.

One of the reasons why I have stressed the importance of listening to your spouse is because many times in a conversation they will express a desire that you can fulfill if you are listening. There have been times my wife or I have mentioned a desire we have and we were able to fulfill that desire because we were listening. We always do our best to meet each other's desires.

For instance, one time my wife mentioned a desire to have a dishwasher in the house. One night while she was at a ladies' meeting at our church, I went to the local appliance store, bought a dishwasher and installed it before she got home. When she arrived and saw the dishwasher, you would have thought I had just given her a million dollars. Well, maybe not quite that much money, but she was certainly happy that I did this for her.

I remember another time when I mentioned in passing how I wanted a Bible from my former pastor, Dr. Jack Hyles. For one of my birthdays she called up my good friend Dr. Russell Anderson and told him how I had always wanted a Bible from Bro. Hyles. She asked him if he had any suggestions. He called her back a couple days later and told her that he gave Bro. Hyles a Bible years ago, and when he died they gave the Bible back to him as a memento. He ended up sending her the Bible with a personal note to me from him as well. When she gave me that Bible it thrilled my heart to know that she went through all the time and effort to meet my desire.

I promise you, when you will spend time and effort trying to meet the needs and desires of your spouse, you will help yourself in winning their heart.

9. Do special things for your spouse just because you love them.

This is different from pampering your spouse in that there are times when you should do something special for them for no other reason than you dearly love them. The only time many people do something for their spouse is on their birthday, anniversary or Christmas. These should not be the only times when you do something for your spouse.

Men, you could buy your wife some flowers at a time other than those expected occasions. You could stop by the store on the way home and buy your wife some chocolates. When she asks you why you did this, then tell her you did it simply because you love her.

Ladies, you could go buy your husband a gift card to his favorite sporting-goods store at a time when he is not expecting it. You could cook him his favorite dessert just because you love him.

Doing special things at off times is a great way to show your love to your spouse. They need to know that you don't just do things for them when it is expected of you, but you do things for them when it is unexpected as well. Yes, be sure to take care of those expected days, but do something special for them at unexpected times just because you love them and want to make them happy. When they see that you are willing to do something special for them at unexpected times, then they will see your attempt to love them.

10. Don't break the heart of your spouse once they give it to you.

I don't know that I can stress this enough. Once you have earned the right for your spouse to give you their heart, then don't break it, for if you break it, you may never get it back. Once Delilah obtained Samson's heart in Judges 16:18, she did not treat it right and ended up breaking his heart and destroying his life.

The heart is a very fragile thing. When the heart is broken, it is very painful. If you have ever had your heart broken by someone whom you gave it to, then you understand what I am saying. When you do something to break the heart of your spouse, you may never be able to gain enough trust to get their heart back. People are usually very protective of their heart. When they give their heart to someone and then that someone carelessly hurts or breaks it, they will usually never give it back to that person. Don't do that to your spouse! If they give you their heart, treat it like a very fragile piece of crystal. Handle it with care for you don't want to break the heart of the one you truly love.

One of the goals in your marriage should be to win the heart of your spouse. Work at it! Pray and ask God that they will give you their heart. Once you have won their heart and they have given it to you, then be very careful not to break it, for if you do you may never gain their heart again.

Chapter 15

Embarrassment; Now or Later

Every marriage will have tense moments which can cause problems. How long you have been married does not keep you from having marital problems. There are those who have been married a few months who have marriage problems, and even those who have been married for several years have marriage problems. Eventually everybody will have some marital problems, albeit some of these problems are very minimal whereas others may be very serious.

Let me make this very clear from the beginning of this chapter, just because you have marital problems does not mean that you are a bad couple or are bad people. Like I previously said, everybody has had to deal with problems in their marriage. The reason why is because you have two sinful human beings involved in marriage. When you have two sinful human beings involved in something together, you are bound to have problems. What you do when those problems come may ultimately determine whether or not your marriage succeeds.

Getting counsel for your marriage can be very embarrassing. It shouldn't be embarrassing though, because everybody at some point has to deal with some problems in marriage. Counsel from the right counselor can certainly get you through your problems much more quickly than trying to handle it by yourselves. If you are not careful, you will avoid getting marriage counseling because of the embarrassment you will face when you have to admit you need help with some problems in your marriage. You have a choice at this point, you can either swallow your pride now and get counseling, or you can avoid the counseling and be embarrassed publicly when you go through a divorce. Being privately embarrassed by getting counseling instead of being openly embarrassed by going through a divorce should be your choice.

The Scripture says in Psalm 73:24, *"Thou shalt guide me with thy counsel, and afterward receive me to glory."* Notice that counseling will guide you. In other words, when you go to get marital counseling, this counsel will help guide your marriage in the proper direction.

Again, God says in Proverbs 15:22, *"Without counsel purposes are disappointed: but in the multitude of counselors they are established."* God is teaching us that the only way to succeed with your purpose is through counseling. Hopefully, the purpose in your marriage is to stay married till death parts you. In order to establish and succeed in that purpose, there are going to be times when you will need to get some counseling. Whatever you do, don't put counseling off until it is too late. Get the counseling you need early enough that the counselor can help you. Let me give you several areas in this chapter that will help you in the area of marital counseling.

First of all, be sure you have the right type of person as your counselor. Using the right counselor could decide whether or not you get the proper advice to help your marriage. Here is some advice to help you in finding the right counselor.

1. Your counselor should be a married person.

I know this may seem obvious, but there are many people who will get advice from someone who has never been married. I think of years ago of a popular figure who was giving counseling on marriage and child rearing who had never been married. The truth is this person had no clue about the differences in a marriage. You would be very wise to choose someone who is happily married as your marriage counselor.

2. Your counselor should be a wise person.

Again, this may seem very obvious, but for the sake of being simplistic, I don't want to overlook the obvious. A person who has been married for a year is probably not the person you want to go to for advice on your marriage. You need someone who is wise enough to give you and your spouse the marital counseling you need.

Of course, a soul winner will be a wise person according to Proverbs 11:30. Whomever you choose to be your counselor should be a soul winner. God gives special wisdom to soul winners. Wisdom comes through experience. Therefore, not only should they be a soul winner, but they should be someone who has been married for several years and who has faced enough situations to be wise enough to give you proper advice.

3. Your counselor should be trustworthy.

When choosing who you want to counsel your marriage, be sure to choose someone who you can trust in two areas. First of all, be sure you can trust them to keep your marital problems private. If the person whom you are considering to counsel your marriage is one who always tends to talk about private conversations, then you might want to choose someone else. You don't need your marital problems broadcasted to everyone. For instance, when I talk to people about their marriage, nobody, not even my wife, knows anything about what was discussed. When someone comes for counseling, they need the assurance that they can open up without having their problems aired to others.

Secondly, be sure that you can trust this counselor to not hold your problems against you. Your counselor should be someone who believes in people being restored. If they can't be trusted not to treat you differently, then I wouldn't go to them. Yet, let me also say that there are some marital problems that will cause you to forfeit the right to do some things for awhile. What I am talking about is making sure your counselor is someone who will put trust in you again after your marital problems are solved.

4. Your counselor should be someone who will tell you what you need to hear.

Don't try to find a counselor who will tell you what you want to hear, but find a counselor who will tell you what you need to hear. At times, a good counselor may have to be very blunt in order to help your marriage. Sometimes they may need to work on you. Don't find someone who is always going to side with you and tell you what you want to hear, instead find a counselor who will give you the counsel that you need to hear.

5. Be sure to use the same counselor.

I have already discussed this in a previous chapter, but let me remind you that it is important that you and your spouse have the same marriage counselor. If you have two separate counselors, then you will get two separate pieces of advice. You don't need disharmony in your marriage counseling. Remember that Amos 3:3 says, *"Can two walk together, except they be agreed?"* Your marital counseling needs to be in agreement so that you and your spouse can walk together in harmony. Be sure you both agree on who you will use for marriage counseling before you ever need it.

Now that we have discussed who to use for marriage counseling, let's discuss some of the signs that show you are in need of counsel. Remember, you are either going to be mildly embarrassed now when you get private counseling, or you will be openly embarrassed when you are going through a divorce. When you see the signs of marriage trouble, get help as soon as possible. Here are some signs of marriage problems that should be addressed in counseling.

1. Poor communication problems

When the only way you and your spouse handle differences in your marriage is through yelling, criticisms, put-downs, arguing or hurtful statements, then you are at a point when you need marital counseling. In this book I have talked extensively about the importance of communication. When the communication breaks down in your marriage, then you need to get counseling so that you can reestablish proper communication. Poor communication between you and your spouse will lead to more severe problems later on. Be sure that when the communication breaks down that you get help to fix whatever is causing the breakdown.

2. Ongoing arguments over unresolved issues

When you find that you and your spouse are constantly arguing over the same issue, then it is time to go and get some help to solve the problem. Apparently you have not been able to solve this issue on your own. For instance, when you are constantly bringing up something from the past, you have an unresolved issue in your marriage. This unresolved issue will continue to fester to the point of explosion if you don't take care of it. Don't let unresolved issues destroy your marriage.

When you find that every argument is over the same issue, and you have not been able to solve it in a reasonable way, then agree to go get some help to solve the problem. Your counselor will help you to resolve the issue so that it doesn't have to come up again. Don't let unresolved issues destroy your marriage. Get help with them before they cause hurts that are hard to heal.

3. An abusive spouse

One of the things an abusive spouse does is blame the other spouse for their abusive actions. The abusive spouse will always blame the abused spouse for driving them to the point where they had to become violent and abusive. The abusive spouse has a hard time taking personal responsibility for their actions.

If your spouse is physically abusing you, **immediately** get help. Don't put your physical safety or the safety of your children at risk by not getting help. Yes, your spouse will threaten that they will harm you or your children more if you go and get help, but you **MUST NOT** allow this to stop you. Your counselor will help you to get the proper help and protection from your spouse. Never think that you are the reason for your spouse physically abusing you.

If you are the one who is physically abusing your spouse, get immediate help. Your anger and rage must be dealt with, and apparently you can't tame them by yourself. If you truly love God and your spouse, you will admit your problem to your counselor and get some help.

4. Disagreement in child rearing

When I am talking about a disagreement in child rearing, I am not talking about every small disagreement you have with your spouse on how to discipline and rear your children. When how to rear or discipline your children becomes so divisive that it causes problems in your marriage, you need to go get some counseling to help solve the problem. Sometimes the counselor can act as a referee to help you and your spouse get on the same page when it comes to the discipline and rearing of your children.

5. Meddling family members

Meddling family members will be one of the hardest things that you will have to deal with in your marriage. It is hard to deal with because you love your family, but you also love your spouse. Many times you will be caught between both sides and will find yourself trying to keep them both happy.

When you have a problem with family members meddling in your marriage, and you can't seem to get them to stop, instead of letting it destroy your marriage, get some help through counseling. Far too many times people let their family members meddle too long in their marriage only to have severe issues come up because they didn't deal with it when it first started to happen. A good counselor will help you and your spouse learn how to deal with meddling family members. Sometimes a counselor will see that you or your spouse are too selfish and don't want anything to do with in-laws. At other times, a counselor will be able to give you good advice on how to handle family members who won't stop meddling. In either case, getting counsel can help you through this situation.

6. Financial hardships

How difficult it is to overcome financial hardships once they come? Once you see you are getting behind in your finances, you need to be sure to swallow your pride and go get some help. Finances will cause stress in a marriage if they are not taken care of properly. When finances become an issue, go get help so you can see the way out. Seeing the way out will help you to overcome undue stress.

7. Withdrawal of your spouse

When your spouse begins to withdraw from you, this would be a good time to go in and get some counseling. There are many reasons why your spouse could be withdrawing from you, and good counseling will help you through this. A spouse who withdraws could be having an affair. A spouse who withdraws could be having health issues that they don't want to disclose. It could also be a major decision they see coming that they don't know how to handle or talk to you about. Whenever your spouse starts withdrawing from you and they won't tell you why, it is a good time to get some advice.

8. An unfaithful spouse

When you find out that your spouse has been unfaithful, you need to immediately get counsel. Your marriage may still be salvaged if you will get help as soon as you find out. Whether the unfaithfulness is a wrong emotional attachment or it is an actual affair, this is a definite time to get counseling. Whether or not the spouse who has committed the wrong is willing to get counsel, you must get some help in dealing with the situation. It won't be easy, but **this is a time when you cannot solve the problem alone**. It is only with counseling that you may salvage your marriage.

9. Substance abuse

Some who read this book may have a spouse that is addicted to alcohol, drugs or some other destructive vice. In situations like these, you must get help for your marriage. Substance abuse is something that can't be quickly overcome. You need counseling to teach you how to deal with your spouse who is addicted, and they will need counseling to help them overcome their addiction. In whichever case you find yourself, be sure to get counseling to help you through this problem.

10. Major decisions in your marriage

When you are about ready to make a major decision in your marriage, be sure to get some advice from your counselor concerning that decision. Some major decisions about which you should get advice is the purchase of a home or car, a new job, or moving the family to a new area of the country. Though this is just a short list, whenever you and your spouse must make a decision that will change the future of your marriage, then you need to get advice from your counselor to be sure your decision is not selfish, but spiritual.

11. Spiritual backsliding

When your spouse begins to backslide, it is not time for you to pull out a sermon and start preaching to them. Many times a concerned spouse will start nagging and preaching only to drive the backslidden spouse further away from them and God. Pray for your spouse if you see them backsliding, but also get some advice from your counselor on how to handle the situation. A backslidden spouse will hurt their marriage, for it will cause a division in their direction. A backslidden spouse will have a different agenda than a spouse who is serving God. This is why you need to get help when your spouse begins to backslide.

In closing, let me give you a few pieces of advice on how to approach your counselor. First of all, get counseling sooner rather than later. It is always easier to take care of a problem in the beginning stages than it is in the progressed stages. Though I believe there is always hope, it is going to be easier and quicker to deal with a problem when it first starts.

Secondly, don't go in to get counseling with your mind made up. When your mind is made up, you might as well not seek counsel. Nobody can help you when you have already made up your mind. Approach counseling with an open heart and mind so that your counselor can be a help to you and your spouse.

Thirdly, approach marital counseling expecting to **personally** change something. Don't go into counseling thinking that your spouse is the one who will have to do all the changing. Most likely both sides caused the problems you are facing. If you will go into counseling expecting to personally change something, this will make it much easier on the one who is counseling you. When your counselor has to fight you to get you to change something, then you are prolonging the problems in your marriage. The quicker you deal with problems by changing the necessary areas of your life, the quicker you will get back to having a happy and joyful marriage.

Lastly, ask God to give your counselor the wisdom to advise you and your spouse. Before you go in, you and your spouse should ask God to show you the areas that you both need to work on, and tell Him that you are willing to change whatever needs to be changed so that your marriage will be what it ought to be. When God sees that a couple is willing to do whatever He wants them to do, then He can help them solve their problems.

Marital counseling is most likely something you will have to have at sometime in your marriage. When you see the signs mentioned in this chapter, immediately go to the counselor whom you and your spouse agreed upon and get help. Remember, you can either be embarrassed a little now or a whole lot later. I think I would rather be a little embarrassed now in a private way than be very embarrassed later in a public way. You will have problems in your marriage, just don't let those problems destroy your marriage before you seek help through counseling.

Chapter 16

Time Alone

Spending time alone is a very important part of the marriage relationship. Though I may be criticized for saying this, being apart for a short time is an important part of making your time together better. If you do what you should do when you are apart from each other, then you will have more quality time when you are together.

Song of Solomon 5:1 says, *"I am come into my garden, my sister, my spouse: I have gathered my myrrh with my spice; I have eaten my honeycomb with my honey; I have drunk my wine with my milk: eat, O friends; drink, yea, drink abundantly, O beloved."* Notice that the spouse in this verse says they *"have gathered."* Notice that this phrase is in the past tense. While they were apart from each other, they gathered things to enjoy while they were with each other. The time apart was wisely used so the time together could be enjoyed and not regretted.

When I talk about spending time alone, I want to divide this up into two segments. I believe it is important that the husband and wife have some time apart from each other so that they can enjoy their time together. Furthermore, I believe it is important for the husband and wife spend time apart from their children and others so they can build their relationship. Both personal time alone and time alone as a couple will help a marriage grow stronger.

PERSONAL TIME

1. Schedule time to be apart from your spouse.

I know this sounds strange, but if a husband and wife are constantly together, it will normally cause a strain on their relationship. Before I go further into this subject, I am not talking about a husband and wife scheduling time to be apart for days and nights at a time. I am talking about being apart during the daytime so that when they come together at night they have a better conversation.

When my wife and I first got married, we spent a lot of time together. At that point in my ministry, I drove to the majority of my revival meetings. My wife was with me most of the time. Even though we spent several hours a day together, we also knew that we needed some time apart to build information to converse about later.

When a couple spends nonstop time together, then they will eventually not have much to talk about, thus hurting the communication within their marriage. Of course, most couples don't have to worry too much about this because of daily work schedules; it still must be mentioned for those who have the capability of being together all the time. If you are one of those couples who has the capability of spending a lot of time together, then it would be wise to schedule time apart so you can gather things about which to converse with each other.

2. While apart, gather information to discuss.

Time apart is a good time to gather information to discuss when you are together. As you are going about your daily business away from your spouse, this is a good time to gather thoughts and information that you will discuss when you are together.

If you are one who has a short memory, then it would be wise to write down things that have happened throughout your day so that you can discuss them with your spouse. The happenings throughout your day should be things you can talk about with your spouse. Don't discuss all the happenings of the day with others, and then get home and not use those happenings as a conversation piece with your spouse.

Many times when my wife and I come together after we have been apart, we will talk about different conversations we have had with others. Likewise, we will discuss exciting things that have happened as well as things that we saw happen around us. One of the biggest reasons for this is because we are best friends, and we would rather talk to each other about all the happenings and thoughts of our days than we would to others.

Don't waste your time apart from your spouse. Use it as a time to gather information to talk about when you come back together.

3. While apart, let your love grow.

Quite often my travel takes me away from home for a couple of days at a time. When I'm away from my wife, I don't want my time away to be a time when my love for my wife cools down. To keep this from happening, I set some time aside in my daily schedule to think about my wife.

For instance, when I think of my wife I always take the time to think of all that she does for me on a daily basis. I think about the good times she and I have had outside of the home. I think about my wife's beauty. I imagine the countenance of her face and her pretty smile. I also think about the sound of her lovely voice. I could go on and on!

The purpose of setting aside time to think about my wife is to keep my love for my wife hot so that when we come together I don't have to rekindle our relationship. I keep the relationship warm in my mind while I'm away.

When you are apart from your spouse, take some time to think about them. Think about what they mean to you. Think about the first time you met and what you thought of them; that is if it was a good first meeting. Think about times when you have had fun together. Think about the times of victory you've had together. I believe you get the picture of what I am talking about. Use your time apart to grow your love for your spouse so that when you come together your love for each other has been kept warm through your thought life.

4. While apart, prepare to be together.

This is important because sometimes a couple will come together and ruin their time together all because they didn't properly prepare themselves to meet each other.

If you have had a tough day, then you need to prepare yourself not to dump on your spouse. Your first meeting together after being apart should not be negative. Coming together should be something that you both enjoy. Prepare yourself by making sure you have a right attitude when you see each other. Don't let your spouse come back to a grumpy or snippy spouse. You've been apart; you should prepare your attitude to meet your spouse. Put aside your day for awhile and make the first meeting with each other an enjoyable time. Don't make the time of coming together a time your spouse really doesn't enjoy because of your attitude. If you do that, then they may start finding excuses to not come home when they should. Work on preparing your attitude for the first meeting after being apart from your spouse.

Let me explain! When I come home from a trip, my dog is always very excited to see me. My wife barely opens the door and the dog is running out the door to come see and greet me with a lick on the hands. I almost have to tell her to calm down because she is so excited when I come home.

Now I would hate to think that my dog greets me better than I greet my wife when I come home. You need to work at making that first time together after being apart an exciting and warm time. It is a choice! If you will prepare yourself for the first greeting, you can greet your spouse with a good attitude. Be sure to make those first few minutes together enjoyable ones.

TIME ALONE AS A COUPLE

1. You need time alone from everyone else.

Your marriage needs time away from the children. There are many couples who never get time alone once the children are born. This is a huge mistake! If your marriage relationship is going to grow as it should, then you must be sure to spend time alone, apart from the children.

Many couples have allowed their children to hurt their marriage because they will never allow themselves to be apart from them. If you are not careful, you will start driving a wedge between your spouse and your children if you don't spend alone time with your spouse. Before your children were born, your spouse had all of your time. I know that once children come there must be a rearrangement of time, but your spouse still needs that time alone with you.

The future of your marriage demands that you spend time alone with each other. Your children will only be in your home for so many years. Once they are gone, if you have not nurtured your relationship with each other, then you will have a gap between you and your spouse that could have been filled if you would have spent time alone during your child-rearing years. Many times couples will separate after the children are gone. One of the main culprits for this is that they didn't nurture their relationship by having time alone when the children were still at home. Let me make this very clear, your marriage relationship is more important than you being with your children all of the time. If your children see that they have parents who are madly in love with each other, then they will have an easier time obeying them. Don't destroy the future of your marriage by not spending time alone right now.

2. "Babysitter" is not a bad word.

There is one word that many couples need to learn and that word is "babysitter." I know that your children are so special that there is nobody good enough to watch them. But let me remind you, for the sake of your marriage you need to learn to let someone watch your children so you and your spouse can spend some time alone.

Of course, you want the babysitter to be someone who is dependable and can take care of emergency situations. This babysitter needs to be someone who can take care of situations without having to call you every five minutes. If they can't, then you need to find yourself another babysitter.

Let me say that your child is not the first child to be so special. Everybody's child is special to them, but your spouse had better be more special. God made children pretty resilient and they can handle being away from you for a few hours or even a night. Don't let your fear of leaving your children with a babysitter keep you from spending time alone with your spouse. Your spouse needs some time alone with you, and your children need you to spend some time alone with each other. So, learn to get a babysitter so this can be accomplished.

3. Schedule a regular time to be alone.

If you are not careful, you will get so busy with life that you will never have time to be alone. If you are going to be successful in spending regular time alone, then you will have to make this a part of your regular schedule.

I think it would be good to have some time alone on a weekly basis. This could be a weekly time when you have a date with your spouse. If you don't like to call it a date, then call it whatever you want to call it, but have some time every week when you spend two or three hours alone with your spouse and away from the children. It would also be good to schedule a night alone at least once a quarter. Of course, if you could do this once a month that would be good as well, but I would advise no less than once a quarter.

This time alone for a night might mean that the children will need to spend the night with their grandparents. It could also mean that you might need to get a hotel room and have the babysitter come over to the house and spend the night at your home with the children. Whatever you do, just be sure that as a couple you have a night away from the children. If you are going to do this, then it will have to be scheduled. If you don't schedule it, then it will never happen.

4. Make your alone time enjoyable.

When you are alone with your spouse, your time needs to be enjoyable or it will become something that you will let fall by the wayside. That means you will probably have to do some planning in order to make your time alone enjoyable.

There are many ways you can make this time alone enjoyable, but if it's going to be enjoyable, then you will have to take some time to plan it. To make it enjoyable for each spouse, then each spouse needs to take time to plan the time apart. To keep both involved, you could both include something that you would like to do with your spouse and try to take something from each other's list. You could also take turns in planning your time alone. One week the husband plans the time alone and the next week the wife does the planning. This way both of you will regularly be doing something that you both enjoy.

Let me also say that when you plan alone time with your spouse, be sure to think of your spouse and not just about yourself. Men, I don't think your wife would enjoy going to the hunting or fishing supply store. Likewise ladies, I know your husband probably doesn't want to go shopping all the time. He won't mind going with you for a short time, but make it short. Whatever you do, make your time enjoyable so that both of you will want to do this on a regular basis. Ask your friends about places and restaurants where they have gone that they enjoyed, and check them out yourself. Don't let your marriage become boring because you do the same thing over and over again. Learn to be creative and make your time together fun and enjoyable.

5. Be alone when you are alone.

This point sounds very strange, but the truth is many times when a couple is alone, they are still not alone. What I mean by this is they still want to answer the cell phone, browse the internet on their phone or check their email. I promise you, those things will still be there when you get home. If you can't ignore your cell phone when you are alone with your spouse, then leave it at home.

Furthermore, you don't need to be calling the babysitter every thirty minutes to be sure that everything is fine. If you can't trust the babysitter to take care of the children the whole time you are gone without calling them, then you probably need to look for another babysitter. The time alone with your spouse is so that you can be alone and enjoy each other. When you're constantly calling the babysitter, answering the phone or checking your email, you are wasting the time that you could be spending with your spouse. Whatever you do, be sure that you are alone when you are alone with your spouse.

Time alone is important for every relationship. God wants us to have time alone with Him to build our relationship together. Now if God feels it's important to have an alone time with us in order to build our relationship, then most certainly you and your spouse need time alone to build your relationship. Don't get so busy that you never have time alone. Be sure to spend time alone on a regular basis with your spouse so that you can nurture and build your relationship.

Chapter 17

Don't Forget to Be Romantic

Go back in your mind to the months when you were dating your spouse and try to remember how romantic you were in your relationship. To be romantic with the person with whom you wanted to marry was not a difficult task. Many of your dates were filled with romantic ideas. Throughout the week you did romantic things for your future spouse all in an effort to win their heart and love over to you. Your dream was to marry them and to continue the romance together for the rest of your life.

The sad part is that many times after a couple has been married for a few years, the romantic side seems to die off. The husband can almost get cold in this area of being romantic. He seems to think that he is married and now he doesn't have to be romantic anymore. The wife gets busy with having to help the children and many times she overlooks the necessity of being romantic with her husband. She gets tired with the chores of keeping up the house and taking care of the children to where she no longer seems to have the energy or desire to be romantic. A couple who becomes like this will adopt the idea that they are married and that their spouse will never leave them, thus neglecting the romance in their marriage.

This loss of the romantic side in a marriage can cause married couples to grow cold and indifferent towards each other. If a couple is not careful, their marriage will become a business partnership because the only thing that holds them together is the contract of the vows that they took.

Your marriage should never lose its romantic side. If you want to keep the romance in your marriage, then you need to continue to be romantic with your spouse. For a couple to stay romantic is not always going to be easy, in fact, it will take hard work, but the rewards of being romantic are great for both husband and wife.

The word "romantic" means, "inclined toward or suggestive of the feeling of excitement and mystery associated with love." The word "romantic" comes from the word "romance." When you look at the word "romantic" you find that it deals with the imagination. In other words, you will never be romantic without having a good imagination. It takes time to think about how you can be romantic with your spouse. The purpose of being romantic with your spouse is to keep the romance in the marriage. The purpose of being romantic with your spouse is to keep your love for each other warm and passionate.

As I have previously stated in this book, the marriage relationship is a picture of the relationship of the church with Christ. The church is the future bride of Christ, and its relationship with Him should mirror the relationship of a husband and wife in their marriage and vice versa. Keeping this thought in mind, when God addressed the church of Ephesus, He said that He was against this church in Revelation 2:4 when He said, *"Nevertheless I have somewhat against thee, because thou hast left thy first love."* In other words, this church lost the romantic side of its love for God. If God was against the church losing its romantic side, then God would be against a marriage losing its romantic side as well. God wants the married couple to continue to be romantic with each other as long as they are married. They must not become like the church of Ephesus who left their first love. Many times you leave something because you forget about it.

174

I want to remind you to be careful that you don't forget to be romantic in your marriage.

Over the next few pages, I want to give you some ideas on how to be romantic with your spouse. Though some of these ideas have already been discussed, I want to reemphasize them in correlation to this chapter with the importance of being romantic.

1. Don't let the attempt to be romantic be one-sided.

Far too many times it is just one side who tries to be romantic hoping that their spouse will respond. It is the responsibility of both you and your spouse to work on this area of being romantic. Don't let your spouse be the only one who is romantic in your marriage. You ought to work on being romantic as well. If you are the one who tries to be romantic and your spouse does not respond back, then don't let their lack of effort stop you from keeping the romance in your marriage.

Many times you can learn how to be romantic with your spouse by watching how they are romantic with you. If they do something romantic for you, it could be their attempt to try to tell you that they would like to have you do the same thing for them. Keep that in mind as I give you ideas later in this chapter.

Furthermore, when your spouse is attempting to be romantic with you, it could be their way of crying out for you to be romantic with them. If they are the only one who is being romantic, then they may begin to wonder if someone else has your attention. Even if you are not the romantic type, then become the romantic type for the sake of your spouse.

2. Keep your appearance sharp.

I will deal with your appearance in a later chapter, but I want to stress that one way you can be romantic is to be clean and sharp for your spouse. Running around all day in your nightgown or torn up blue jeans is not very romantic. If anybody ought to see you dressed sharp it should be your spouse. Your spouse should feel that you love them enough to be clean, shaven, groomed and dressed sharp for them. Keeping your appearance sharp is a good start in being romantic with your spouse.

3. Use loving words with each other.

The husband in Song of Solomon said about his wife in Song of Solomon 2:10, *"My beloved spake, and said unto me, Rise up, my love, my fair one, and come away."* Notice the loving words he used in describing his wife. He did not call her the "old lady," but he said loving words to her.

I believe it is very important to say loving words to each other in order to keep your marriage romantic. When you study the book of Song of Solomon, you will see that they had loving names that they called each other. Having a loving name that you call your spouse is another way to be romantic. Both you and your spouse should choose some loving names for each other. Likewise, with your words you should always be loving in order to keep your marriage romantic.

4. Write love notes.

It would be good on a regular basis to write your spouse love notes. With today's technology, you can easily let your spouse know throughout the day that you are thinking about them. Through a text or email, you can become romantic with your spouse. You could leave them a card around the house or in their briefcase, purse or lunch box. This is just one way you could be romantic with your spouse. Don't think that they won't appreciate you doing this. They will notice this action whether or not they mention it to you. Let me also say, if your spouse leaves you notes like this, it would be good for you to respond later on with a note to them or a simple "thank you" for thinking about you.

5. Regularly display affection towards each other.

In Song of Solomon 1:2, the wife shows her desire for her husband's affection by saying, *"Let him kiss me with the kisses of his mouth: for thy love is better than wine."* In Song of Solomon 2:6, we see that the husband gave affection to his wife when it says, *"His left hand is under my head, and his right hand doth embrace me."* The couple in this marriage regularly showed their affection to each other.

One way to be romantic with your spouse is to regularly show affection towards them. Kissing should be a regular diet in your marriage. Don't ever push away the kisses of your spouse. Kissing your spouse should not only be done when you are alone, but even when you leave each other in public. Don't be ashamed of your spouse! You should be thankful that they would want to show affection towards you this way. I believe it would be wise to be passionate in your kissing as well. Of course this type of kissing should be reserved for private times.

Likewise, be romantic with each other by holding hands. Don't be the couple who is never seen holding hands in public. When you go somewhere together, walk in holding hands. When you're in the car, if your spouse wants to hold your hand then don't turn them down. It didn't bother you before you were married, and it dead sure shouldn't bother you now.

6. Plan special occasions with your spouse.

The husband planned a special occasion for his wife in Song of Solomon 2:4 when it says, *"He brought me to the banqueting house, and his banner over me was love."* Notice it says he planned a special meal for his wife. Also, when she arrived at the place where the meal was to be served, he had a special banner made for his wife. This is a good example of a husband being romantic with his wife.

As a married couple, you should plan special occasions when you and your spouse go somewhere alone. Maybe the husband should plan to take the wife out for a romantic dinner to a special restaurant. Maybe the wife could plan a romantic dinner at the house for her husband and send the children away for the evening. You could also just go out for a picnic together in the park or in the woods somewhere. You could also plan a special night away in a fancy hotel with your spouse. This is all an attempt to stay romantic in your marriage.

7. Buy your spouse special gifts.

By now, you should know some things that your spouse really likes. Too many times the only time your spouse gets something special from you is on their birthday or your anniversary. Buying special gifts for no other reason than that you love them is a very romantic gesture.

There are many gifts you can buy your spouse. Some ideas could be some chocolate candies that they like. You could get them a fruit bouquet that is delivered to the house or their place of employment. Maybe you could have a special bouquet of flowers delivered to your wife with a love note included. You could also go shopping and buy them something they really like and give it to them as a gift when they get home. These are not the only things you can do to be romantic, but you should constantly search and look for gifts that you can buy your spouse every once in awhile.

8. Have fun and laugh with each other.

There is something romantic about having fun and laughing with your spouse. Let me be very blunt with some of you, loosen up and enjoy life a bit. Sometimes you just need to let your hair down a bit and enjoy having fun with your spouse. Who better to have fun with than the one to whom you are married? There is something very romantic about having fun with the person you love. Though this may not be very "smoochy," it is needed in every marriage. You better learn to have times when you laugh with your spouse because there will be plenty of times when you will cry together. When you can cry, laugh and have fun together, you will find this can be very romantic.

9. Take walks and drives together.

Sometime at night, go on a drive with your spouse and look out over the city lights. Find a place to park and enjoy being with your spouse. Maybe in the daytime you could take a nice drive down the ocean shoreline or through some wooded forest together. This is a good way to just spend time alone with each other. Take your time and don't be in such a big hurry. Hey, maybe you could get lost together for a while; you always wanted to get lost without your chaperone when you were dating, so take advantage of it now.

Likewise, take time to go on a walk with your spouse. Take a walk through the neighborhood together on a sunny day and just enjoy being with each other. Sometimes being romantic is just spending some time alone with your spouse and talking. Taking a walk with them is a good way to do this.

10. Take mini-dates with your spouse.

On the spur of the moment, you should go somewhere with your spouse to spend some time with them. You could go to the coffee shop and enjoy a coffee or espresso with them. You could also go to the ice cream shop and share a shake or ice cream together.

When I talk about having a mini-date, I am simply talking about taking a short time together when you can be alone. You should take advantage of every opportunity possible to be with your spouse. This mini-date could happen on their lunch break with you meeting them somewhere quickly, or it could be that you show up at their break time with a cup of coffee to spend ten minutes with them. Maybe the children happen to be gone for a couple of hours on church activities, then run over and have a mini-date together.

11. Plan a surprise for your spouse.

Use your imagination, but be creative in this area. Find something that you can do to let them know that you can't wait to see them that night when they get home. This should not be something you do all the time or else it won't be special, but you should every once in awhile surprise them. Ladies, you can certainly surprise your husband in your own way, and men, it might be that you simply use one of your vacation days and surprise your wife with a day at home. All I'm going to say in this area is if you are going to be romantic, then you will need to get creative in order to surprise them.

12. Save for a special trip.

Sometime in your marriage you should save money for a special trip together. Work together at saving money so that you and your spouse can take a trip that you have always wanted to take.

Take a second honeymoon and go to a cabin in the mountains for a few days. Maybe you can save enough money to take a cruise together or spend some time at a bed and breakfast or beachfront hotel. If you plan wisely, you can save yourself hundreds of dollars by doing these in the off-peak season. Do some research, and then start planning for that special trip. When you take the trip, make it special and plan many romantic things you can do together.

13. Baby your spouse when they are sick.

Notice what happens in Song of Solomon 2:7, *"I charge you, O ye daughters of Jerusalem, by the roes, and by the hinds of the field, that ye stir not up, nor awake my love, till he please."* I don't know if the husband was sick or just very tired, but what I do notice is that the wife was trying to take care of her husband during this time. In all reality, she was babying him.

Every person likes to be babied when they don't feel well. Men especially are the biggest babies when they are sick. Whenever your spouse gets sick, use that time to give them special attention and baby them. It is a very romantic act on your part to baby your spouse when they don't feel well.

14. Do a home project together.

Sometimes you can be romantic by doing a project around the house together. Instead of making it a "honey do list," why don't you make it a romantic project that you do together? When you work together you are building a tighter bond with each other. The closer you are to your spouse the more romantic these projects can become. Let the small remodeling project that will only take a day be a romantic day of you and your spouse working together to get it done. There is something about looking at a finished project that you worked together to complete. The satisfaction of doing something together is romantic in its own sense.

15. Keep the bedroom romantic.

Of all the places in a house that ought to be romantic, it should be the bedroom where you and your spouse sleep. You will notice that the couple in Song of Solomon made their bedroom have a romantic atmosphere in Song of Solomon 3:7 when it says, *"Behold his bed, which is Solomon's; threescore valiant men are about it, of the valiant of Israel."* The wife is talking about the bed and how it was built. Her husband worked on making sure their bedroom had a romantic atmosphere.

It is highly important for your bedroom to have a romantic atmosphere. If any room in the house is going to have some money invested in it, make sure that your bedroom is that room. Make the atmosphere in your bedroom as romantic as you can through the lighting and colors. This will help to keep that romantic spirit in your house and will keep the romance between each other special.

16. Flirt with each other.

You should never stop flirting with each other. This makes marriage fun, exciting and fresh. The husband in Song of Solomon talked about how his wife flirted with him in Song of Solomon 4:9 when he said, *"Thou hast ravished my heart, my sister, my spouse; thou hast ravished my heart with one of thine eyes, with one chain of thy neck."* Notice how he said that his wife ravished his heart with her eyes. Most likely this is talking about her winking at him as she flirted with him.

Make it a regular part of your marriage to flirt with your spouse. Instead of wasting your energy trying to impress someone else's spouse, you should spend time flirting with your spouse. Just because you have been married for several years does not give you a right to stop flirting with your spouse. Make it a habit to flirt and tease your spouse. This will help to add romance to your marriage.

Just because you have been married for many years does not give you an excuse to not be romantic. You should constantly work at being romantic in your marriage. Yes, it will take work and imagination, but it is worth it.

Every idea I have given in this chapter is just that, an idea. You need to get creative and be sure that you don't forget to be romantic. Take some time every week to think of how you can be romantic in your marriage. Don't throw cold water on your spouse when they attempt to be romantic with you. Encourage them and be a part of it. Remember that imagination is a part of the definition of romantic. So, use your imagination and constantly find new ways that you can be romantic with your spouse.

Chapter 18

Defraud Not

It is common for married couples to face problems in their intimate life. Though many would not admit it, when you start dealing with people who are experiencing problems in their marriage, many times this subject will come up.

This is certainly a very touchy subject to deal with in the pages of a book. I personally do not believe that it is proper to become graphic concerning the intimate life of a married couple. In fact, in this chapter, I will try to be very discreet in how I discuss this subject. I realize there are young people who are not married who may pick up this book and start reading it, and I don't want to open their minds to temptation. I personally feel that a married couple will understand what I am talking about without my having to go into great detail.

With this in mind, let me say that the Scriptures make it very clear that God is for a husband and wife being intimate with each other. Hebrews 13:4 says, *"Marriage is honourable in all, and the bed undefiled: but whoremongers and adulterers God will judge."* First of all, you will notice that God says the bed is for the husband and wife. He makes this clear when He says that He will judge the whoremonger and adulterer. By the way, this makes it very clear that intimacy before marriage is wrong as well. Secondly, God wants the husband and wife to be intimate with each other. That is why

He said the *"bed is undefiled."* In God's eyes, He feels it is proper for the husband and wife to enjoy each other intimately.

God says in 1 Corinthians 7:5, *"Defraud ye not one the other, except it be with consent for a time, that ye may give yourselves to fasting and prayer; and come together again, that Satan tempt you not for your incontinency."* The word *"defraud"* means "to deprive of a right; to wrongfully withhold from another what is due him; to wrongfully prevent one from obtaining what he may rightfully claim; to cheat." Defraud is a strong word for God to use regarding the withholding of intimacy from your spouse. In other words, God is calling you a fraud if you don't meet the intimate needs of your spouse. By using the word *"defraud"* to show the need of intimacy between a married couple, God makes it very clear that it is the right of each spouse to be able to have their intimate needs met **whenever** those needs arise. To not meet your spouse's needs is a fraudulent act on the part of the spouse who isn't willing to meet those needs.

Let me give you several thoughts concerning intimacy in your marriage. I want you to remember as you read these thoughts that God expects every married couple to enjoy each other in this area.

1. Your body belongs to God.

God says in 1 Corinthians 6:19-20, *"What? know ye not that your body is the temple of the Holy Ghost which is in you, which ye have of God, and ye are not your own? For ye are bought with a price: therefore glorify God in your body, and in your spirit, which are God's."* You will notice God says that He purchased your body. Therefore, if God purchased your body, then your body no longer belongs to you, but to Him.

Because God owns your body, He has the right to tell you what to do with it. Because God owns your body, you should never do anything with it that God would not approve of. As owner of your body, God has the right to do what He wants with your body.

2. God has given His authority of your body to your spouse.

What a powerful fact that God would give His rights to your body over to your spouse. God says in 1 Corinthians 7:4, *"The wife hath not power of her own body, but the husband: and likewise also the husband hath not power of his own body, but the wife."* Look at who has the power over your body; it is your spouse who owns the rights to your body. In other words, when you got married you signed over the rights of your body to your spouse. Your spouse has a God given right to enjoy your body, for God has given them this authority.

According to the verses above, if your spouse desires to be intimate with you, then you have no right to withhold that intimacy from them, for they have power over your body. For you to try and take your body from your spouse is to take something that does not belong to you. In spite of what society may believe, your body belongs to your spouse and not to you.

3. The act of intimacy between husband and wife is honourable.

Hebrews 13:4 says, *"Marriage is honourable in all, and the bed undefiled: but whoremongers and adulterers God will judge."* You will notice in this verse that God says marriage is *"...honourable in all..."* This includes the act of intimacy between the husband and wife.

Sometimes a couple has worked so hard at staying pure until the day when they were married, that once they are married they have a hard time enjoying their spouse. Let me make this very clear, there is nothing wrong with a married couple being intimate with each other as often as they want. Let me make this clearer if I can, now that you are married it is just as wrong for you to withhold from your spouse as it was for you to enjoy them before marriage. God says that it is honourable for you to enjoy your spouse, so for you not to enjoy them would be dishonourable to God. I am sure that you don't want to dishonour God.

4. Intimacy is only between the husband and wife.

Again, look at the verse above when God says that *"Marriage is honourable in all..."* We have already discussed in this book that marriage is between a man and a woman. According to the Scriptures this man and woman are to cleave to each other and to no one else.

Therefore, whatever goes on between the husband and wife is no one else's business. The act of intimacy between a husband and wife is not to be discussed with anyone else. It is only between the husband and wife. You should not discuss your intimate life with others, for that is only for you and your spouse. Be sure to keep your intimate life private and never discuss any aspect of it with others.

5. Intimate fulfillment protects the marriage from affairs.

I want you to look at two verses to see how the act of intimacy will protect your marriage from affairs. 1 Corinthians 7:5 says, *"Defraud ye not one the other, except it be with consent for a time, that ye may give yourselves to fasting and prayer; and come together again, that Satan tempt you not for your incontinency."* You will notice that God warns you that a lack of intimacy will lead to temptation. God knows that if a husband and wife are meeting each other's intimate needs, then they won't be looking around to have their needs met by someone else. When you withhold from your spouse, they are then tempted and may end up having an affair with someone else, and you would be partly to blame. I know that some may get upset with this statement, but God plainly shows that a lack of intimacy will lead to temptation. Ultimately everyone is responsible for their own actions, and each of us are responsible for controlling ourselves. Even if their spouse does not meet their physical needs, the spouse who withholds those intimate needs is guilty of pushing their spouse toward an affair.

The Scriptures say in Song of Solomon 8:10, *"I am a wall, and my breasts like towers: then was I in his eyes as one that found favour."* In this verse, you will find that by the wife meeting the needs of her husband she found favour with him. In other words, simply by meeting her husband's physical needs she kept his eyes on her and not on anyone else. You can keep your spouse from looking around if you will meet their intimate needs. Regularly meeting each other's physical needs will help protect your marriage from an affair.

You must be careful that you don't allow coldness in the area of intimacy to become a tool that Satan could use to destroy your marriage. Satan knows if you withhold intimacy from your spouse that they are more vulnerable to the temptations of others. Therefore, be sure to meet their physical needs so that you don't become the tool that Satan uses against your spouse.

6. Don't hide yourself from your spouse.

As you read the verse above, you will see that the wife allowed her husband to see her. By her meeting this need, God gave the husband eyes for his wife alone. You must not hide your body from your spouse because you think your body looks ugly. God will give your spouse eyes for you, so meet those needs.

Furthermore, we must remember that God says that our body does not belong to us. Therefore, if your spouse wants to see you, then you have no right to hide yourself from them. In Song of Solomon 2:14, the wife said about her husband, *"O my dove, that art in the clefts of the rock, in the secret places of the stairs, let me see thy countenance, let me hear thy voice; for sweet is thy voice, and thy countenance is*

187

comely." It is important for you to understand that your spouse needs to see you just as much as they need to be intimate with you. Be careful about hiding yourself from your spouse. Though you may think that you are uncomely, God has given your spouse eyes for you, so let them enjoy seeing you.

7. The degree of intimacy is between the husband and wife.

Let me again refer to Hebrews 13:4 when it says that *"Marriage is honourable in all, and the bed undefiled..."* What the husband and wife do with each other is completely up to them and no one else. You and your spouse need to agree on what you will enjoy with each other. As long as what you want to do does not go against Scripture, then according to the Scriptures it is perfectly fine. The husband and wife alone should determine what is acceptable within the bounds of their intimate relationship.

8. Each spouse needs his or her fulfillment.

Song of Solomon 4:16 says, *"...Let my beloved come into his garden, and eat his pleasant fruits."* It is important to notice that here the wife wanted her husband to enjoy everything he was to enjoy with her.

Let me be frank with you and simply say that you should not be selfish about your physical needs being met. Just because your intimate needs were met does not mean your spouse had their needs met. Both husband and wife need to be very sensitive to make sure both are getting their intimate needs met. Do what you can to be sure that both spouse's needs are being met during intimacy.

9. Your lack of desire is a lack of thought.

Song of Solomon 4:9 says, *"Thou hast ravished my heart, my sister, my spouse; thou has ravished my heart with one of thine eyes, with one chain of thy neck."* In order to be

188

ravished with your spouse, you must be thinking of them. The word *"ravished"* means "to be carried away." This husband was saying that he was carried away with his spouse.

If you have no desire to partake in the intimate acts of marriage, then that is due to a lack of thought. I know you may say, "That is all they think about." Well, if you would think about it, then maybe you would desire it as well. Stop thinking of intimacy as an obligation to obey God! Your spouse is not turned on when you do what you have to do just to be obedient to the Scriptures. Being intimate with your spouse is the right thing to do, and according to the Scriptures it is honourable. Therefore, you would desire intimacy if you would think about it in a positive manner. Don't make your spouse go without their needs being met just because you won't think about being intimate with them. Spend some time thinking about being intimate with your spouse, and you will probably find that you will desire it as well.

10. Out-lure the other person.

Proverbs 7:16 says, *"I have decked my bed with coverings of tapestry, with carved works, with fine linen of Egypt."* In this verse, the strange woman was trying to lure this young man into her house. She was telling him all that she had done to prepare for him. Her whole purpose was to lure him in to get some enjoyment that was not rightfully hers.

You better understand that there are people out there trying to lure your spouse so they can be intimate with them. One of the best ways to keep this from happening is to out-lure them. You need to go all-out to lure your spouse in. Don't let someone else be more romantic and loving toward your spouse than you are. Let your spouse feel as if you want them. Lure them in ways that only you know will entice them. Listen, you are their spouse, so you should be as creative as you can in this area. Don't let a whore do a better job than you of luring your spouse. Simply out-lure the other person.

11. Be thoughtful of your spouse.

There are times in your marriage when you will have to withhold from being intimate with each other. God talks about this in 1 Corinthians 7:5 when He says not to defraud your spouse *"...except it be with consent for a time..."* There will be times when your spouse just will not feel like being intimate. You should be thoughtful of them, as surely this is not a regular occurrence. If they are sick, be thoughtful and understand that you should withhold yourself until they feel better.

Let me also say that you should not always use illness, lack of desire, or not being "in the mood" as an excuse. It may work once or twice, but eventually your excuses will get old. Be careful about always having an excuse as to why you don't want to be intimate with your spouse. Only ask them to wait if you honestly feel it's necessary.

12. Don't get too busy.

With the schedules that husbands and wives keep, it can be easy to never have time to enjoy each other. Sometimes work schedules conflict, and you don't have any time to enjoy each other. If you find that you are so busy that you use it as an excuse to not be intimate, then you need to schedule some time to enjoy each other. I know this doesn't sound romantic, but at the very least your needs will be met, and that is important.

13. Get medical help if needed.

There are some who have not been able to be intimate because of physical ailments. If this is your case, then you need to talk to a doctor and see if it is a physical problem for which there is help. Though this may be embarrassing to bring up to your doctor, you will do your spouse a big favor by taking care of any physical issues that keep you from enjoying intimacy. Likewise, some withhold from their spouse because of their lack of desire. A doctor can treat this problem as well. You know if you are withholding from your spouse because of a physical reason. If a physical reason is the problem, then swallow your pride and go talk to your doctor. You are not the first person to have physical problems that keep you from meeting the needs of your spouse.

14. If needed, get rest.

If the reason why you are not meeting the intimate needs of your spouse is because you are too tired, then you do what you can to get enough rest so that you do desire intimacy. I know that when you are tired it is not always easy to have the energy to enjoy intimacy. So to avoid this, get the rest you need so you have the energy necessary to be intimate with your spouse. If you have to take a nap during the day to be rested, then take a nap, but don't use being tired as your excuse for not meeting the intimate needs of your spouse.

15. Marriage problems are likely the result of an intimacy problem.

Years ago I was talking to a preacher who told me how he counseled couples who were having marriage problems. He said that he would tell the couple to go home, and for the next week enjoy each other intimately as much as they could, and if they still had problems, then to come back and he would help them through their problems. This pastor told me that he rarely had a couple come back after following that advice.

There is a reason why most of those couples rarely came back and that is because many problems in marriage can be traced back to a lack of the physical needs being met. Enjoying each other intimately will solve many of your marriage problems. Let me make this very clear, **both** husband and wife need to be intimate. The act of intimacy is a stress release for both, and without that release you will have problems with each other. Both will become frustrated if they do not have their physical needs met. You can surely avoid many problems in your marriage simply by following the command of God to not defraud your spouse.

16. Withholding from your spouse is fraudulent.

Let me remind you that 1 Corinthians 7:5 says, *"Defraud ye not one the other, except it be with consent for a time..."* Let's just be realistic about this, part of the reason you got married was so that you could enjoy the act of intimacy. If the only reason you got married was to be best friends, then you didn't need to get married, for you could do that without being married. One of the reasons people get married is so that they can scripturally enjoy each other in an intimate way.

For you to withhold from your spouse after knowing that intimacy is one of the reasons for marriage is fraudulent. In other words, you are a cheat if you withhold from your spouse. There are some who brag about not meeting the physical needs of their spouse, and that is wrong. If your spouse desires to be intimate with you, then you are to meet that need. To not meet that need is a sin against God and your spouse.

In closing, let me say that God commands the husband and wife to be intimate with each other. God created us with that desire, and we should do everything in our power to be sure that the physical needs of our spouse are always met. Don't let a lack in this area be the cause of friction in your marriage. Don't let a lack in this area drive your marriage to divorce. Your spouse has a God given right to enjoy you. You should make sure that nobody else can give your spouse something that you have not given to them. Your body belongs to your spouse; don't defraud them of what is rightfully theirs.

Chapter 19

Handling Disagreements

When a young couple gets married, they can't imagine themselves having sharp disagreements. Most young couples believe that they will be the exception to the rule. They soon find out, after a few months of marriage, that disagreements do come, and many times these disagreements end up causing major marital strife.

The goal of your marriage is to learn, in a proper manner, how to handle your disagreements. Whether you like it or not, disagreements will crop up in your marriage. There are many reasons why there are disagreements in a marriage. For instance, you and your spouse each have a unique personality. Your personality will not always agree with the personality of your spouse. Also, disagreements happen because of the difference in gender. I know that you already know this, but men and women do not think alike. This difference in the thinking process can cause disagreements. Furthermore, you and your spouse have different routines and ways of doing things. Especially, when you first get married, the routines of you and your spouse are very different. Until you learn to adjust to the routine of your spouse, your routine can certainly cause many sharp disagreements.

Your goal in your marriage should be to resolve any disagreements as quickly as possible. The longer you let your disagreements go unresolved, the more they will fester ill feelings towards your spouse. If your disagreements are not quickly resolved, they can fester into a full-blown problem. You don't want this to happen in your marriage. This is why it is important to handle your disagreements quickly and properly. Let me give you several pieces of advice on how to handle disagreements in your marriage.

1. Calm down

When you and your spouse have a disagreement, the first thing you should do is calm down. Reacting to your disagreement will most likely end up causing you to do some things you will regret later. Taking time to calm down is always better than speaking your mind.

God says in Proverbs 16:32, *"He that is slow to anger is better than the mighty; and he that ruleth his spirit than he that taketh a city."* Notice that God talks about being *"slow to anger."* God is teaching that before you start responding to disagreements with your spouse, you need to get control of your spirit and rule it instead of it ruling you. The best way to accomplish this is to take some time to calm down before you and your spouse begin to deal with the problem.

I have learned that if I am hot over a disagreement the best way for me to cool down is to walk away. I would rather walk away and get control of my spirit than do something harsh that I will regret later. This is where many people find themselves saying and doing things they wished they had never done. In the heat of the moment, their spirit is controlling them, and they end up saying words they should have never said, or some will even get physical with their spouse. Both of these things can be avoided if you will simply take time to calm down when you disagree with your spouse.

2. Take care of the problem at hand.

One of the mistakes people make when they have disagreements is they try to deal with every problem they have instead of dealing with the disagreement at hand. When they start doing this, they end up with a bigger problem than they originally had.

The Scriptures say concerning disagreements in Matthew 18:15, *"Moreover if thy brother shall trespass against thee, go and tell him his fault between thee and him alone: if he shall hear thee, thou hast gained thy brother."* Notice that when the disagreement happens, God tells us to go to our brother and *"...tell him his fault..."* God is teaching us in this verse to deal with one problem at a time. The word *"fault"* is singular. God didn't say to go tell your brother his faults. He said to deal with the one fault you currently have.

In your marriage, you need to learn to deal with the fault at hand. You will have a better chance of resolving the current disagreement if you deal with that issue alone.

3. Don't bring up past problems.

I follow up the previous point with this point because it is important when you are having a disagreement with your spouse that you leave the past out of your discussions. First of all, the past problem was supposed to be resolved. Secondly, bringing up the past does not help you take care of your current situation. The only reason why you would bring up the past in a disagreement is because you feel like you are losing the argument. Bringing up the past will only cause more resentment towards each other in your attempt to resolve your disagreement.

When dealing with past problems with others, God commands us in Ephesians 4:32, *"And be ye kind one to another, tenderhearted, forgiving one another, even as God for Christ's sake hath forgiven you."* You will notice in this verse that God tells us to forgive each other the same way that He forgave us. All you have to remember is that when God forgave us of our sins they were gone forever. God never brings our past up to us; He only brings up our future. The only one who will bring up our past is Satan because he is the accuser of the brethren.

When you start accusing your spouse by bringing up the past, then you are copying the works of Satan. You must realize that bringing up the past is unproductive in resolving disagreements. When you and your spouse disagree on something, you need to leave the past alone and deal with the present. When you only deal with the present you can solve the problem a whole lot easier.

4. Don't seek to win.

Your goal in handling the disagreement you have with your spouse should be to resolve the issue and not simply to win. When your desire is to win, then you are on a dangerous path of never resolving disagreements, which will eventually lead to marital problems that may not be able to be resolved.

Let me remind you that you and your spouse are a team. Team members are not to try and defeat each other; team members are to seek to work together. If one spouse or the other is constantly trying to win every argument or disagreement, then you will find that you will rarely get along.

Let me remind you of a verse I have used often in this book, Amos 3:3, *"Can two walk together, except they be agreed?"* The goal of your marriage is to be able to live peaceably together. The only way to accomplish this is for you and your spouse to agree on matters and each not seek to win. Stop trying to win when you are handling a disagreement and seek to resolve it so that you can walk peaceably together.

5. Admit you're wrong.

First of all let me plainly state that most of the time you and your spouse are both wrong in some way. It always takes two sides to argue. If one side is not willing to argue, then there will be no argument.

One of the mistakes that commonly happens in marital relationships is one spouse will never admit their wrong in the disagreement. Yes, one spouse may be more responsible for the disagreement, but certainly there is wrong on both sides.

Instead of always trying to get your spouse to admit their wrong, you need to be the one who admits your wrong. Every instance in the Scriptures when someone was wrong, in order to get that situation resolved, they had to admit their wrong. Likewise, you need to admit your wrong instead of waiting for your spouse to say where they were wrong. Let me ask you this question, when was the last time you admitted to your spouse that you were wrong? I know that you will have to swallow your pride, but admitting your wrong will go a long way toward resolving disagreements in your marriage.

6. Stop blaming and take responsibility for your actions.

Another problem you find when couples are having disagreements is that they constantly want to blame something or someone else for their wrong. Many times it is hard as adults to admit that we are the cause and not someone else.

God says in Romans 14:12, *"So then every one of us shall give account of himself to God."* I want you to see that when it comes to your actions, God will hold you accountable for what you have done. God will not allow you to blame everyone else for what you have done because ultimately you are responsible for your own actions.

In your marriage, you are responsible for your actions. Just because your spouse does wrong does not give you the right to do wrong. Just because your parent's marriage was not right does not give you an excuse for the wrongs that you commit against your spouse. I get weary of people blaming everyone else for their actions; take responsibility for your own actions. Until you stop blaming everyone else for your wrongs, you will never resolve your disagreements.

7. Don't yell!

For these next two points, let me remind you what Proverbs 16:32 says, *"He that is slow to anger is better than the mighty; and he that ruleth his spirit than he that taketh a city."* Remember, we are to rule our own spirit instead of our spirit ruling us.

When you have a disagreement with your spouse, yelling will not resolve the problem. In fact, the only thing that yelling will do is escalate the feelings and make the problem worse. Yelling starts with someone raising their voice. When one raises their voice then the other starts to raise theirs as well. Before long you have two adults yelling at each other just like children.

The only reason why you yell in a disagreement is because you have lost control of your spirit. Furthermore, when someone starts yelling directly at you, human tendency is to stop listening. When you and your spouse get into a shouting match, neither one of you are listening to each other. When no one is listening, then you have no chance of resolving your disagreement. Instead, calm down and get your spirit under control so you can talk to each other in a calm matter.

8. Don't get physical.

Again, referring to Proverbs 16:32, you are commanded to keep your spirit under control. If you don't keep your spirit under control, then most likely you will not keep your body under control. Before a person ever loses control of their body they lose control of their spirit. This is why it is important to keep your spirit under control.

With that said, being physical with your spouse is **NEVER** acceptable! I don't care what your spouse has done; you should never strike your spouse. I say this to both the wife and the husband. Though the majority of the time the husband is the aggressor in this area, there are times when the wife is the one who gets physical in the relationship.

Men, you are not much of a man if you strike your wife. According to 1 Peter 3:7, your wife is the weaker vessel. If you abuse your wife, you are nothing more than a bully. Learn to get your emotions under control! It is never right for a man to hit a woman!

Ladies, just as it is wrong for your husband to strike you, it is wrong for you to get abusive with your husband. Just because you know your husband won't hit you back does not give you a right to slap or hit him. Your husband should never strike you, and you should never strike him.

Lastly, don't get physical in disagreements by throwing things at each other. It is childish and wrong to throw things at each other during a disagreement. Though you may not physically touch your spouse with your hands, throwing things at them is just as much abuse as it is to physically hit them. Getting physical in any way during a disagreement is never acceptable!

9. Seek to move from having a disagreement to solving the problem.

When you have disagreements with your spouse, your goal should be to move as quickly as you can from the disagreement stage to solving the problem that caused the disagreement. The goal in Matthew 18:15 was to solve the disagreement. Look again at what it says, *"Moreover if thy brother shall trespass against thee, go and tell him his fault between thee and him alone: if he shall hear thee, thou hast gained thy brother."* When this verse talks about hearing you, it is talking about the two of you solving your problem. The goal in this verse was to settle the disagreement by solving the problem.

When you and your spouse are having a disagreement, you need to move as quickly as you can towards solving the problem. The best way to move towards problem solving is for both sides to listen to each other. In the verse mentioned earlier, God put the emphasis on hearing. Instead of you and your spouse speaking at the same time, each of you need to learn to stop and listen to what the other is saying. Listen, you know you disagree, so stop using your conversation to blame, and use it to solve the problem. When you and your spouse disagree, learn to ask what you can do to resolve the issue.

10. If you can't resolve a disagreement, get counseling.

Matthew 18:16 says, *"But if he will not hear thee, then take with thee one or two more, that in the mouth of two or three witnesses every word may be established."* This verse is talking about getting help when two parties cannot resolve a disagreement by themselves.

Likewise, when you and your spouse cannot resolve a disagreement, then you need to schedule some time with your pastor for some marital counseling. Because you can't resolve the issue between the two of you, then you need to let your pastor act as a referee in resolving the problem. He will not only act as a referee, but his counsel can advise you on how to avoid that problem again. Don't be so filled with pride that you won't get help when you have disagreements that the two of you cannot resolve.

11. Avoid disagreements by avoiding the cause of a disagreement.

Sometimes we know what causes some of the disagreements in our marriage. Many times you can avoid disagreements by avoiding what causes the disagreement. God says in 1 Thessalonians 5:22, *"Abstain from all appearance of evil."* God is teaching us in this verse to avoid those things that cause us to do evil.

If you know something irritates your spouse, then avoid doing it so that you can avoid disagreement. If you know of something that your spouse does that irritates you, then avoid that situation if possible. You may have to give up something you like in order to avoid that irritation, but that would be better than living your marriage in a constant state of disagreement. Just like you would avoid poison ivy, avoid the cause that leads to disagreements in your marriage. Learn what causes the disagreements in your marriage, and avoid those irritants.

12. Don't finish your day with unresolved disagreements.

God warns us in Ephesians 4:26, *"Be ye angry, and sin not: let not the sun go down upon your wrath:"* God wants us to do everything in our power to resolve issues before the day is over.

It is very unhealthy for your marriage and for you physically to go to sleep with unresolved anger and disagreement. You won't sleep well when you go to sleep steaming about something that your spouse has done. Do what you can to resolve every issue before you go to sleep.

The biggest reason why you should try to resolve disagreements before you go to sleep is because the result of unresolved disagreements is resentment. If you make it a habit to go to sleep with unresolved issues, then you will begin to find that you and your spouse will start harboring resentment towards each other. There is no place for resentment in marriage. You can avoid allowing resentment to get its grip on your marriage by resolving your disagreements before you go to sleep.

13. Settle one battle at a time.

Don't try to win the whole war at one time. Instead, take care of one issue at a time. When you start trying to tackle every problem you have with your spouse at one time, you will end up ruining your relationship and may end up losing your marriage.

The best way to settle disagreements with your spouse is to deal with the problem at hand, and only deal with one disagreement at a time. Settle your current disagreement and then give your marriage some time to heal before you start trying to tackle the next one.

14. Be willing to forgive.

Matthew 18:21-22 says, *"Then came Peter to him, and said, Lord, how oft shall my brother sin against me, and I forgive him? till seven times? Jesus saith unto him, I say not unto thee, Until seven times: but, Until seventy times seven."* God is teaching in this verse the importance of a person always be willing to forgive someone who has wronged them. In any relationship, forgiveness must constantly be available in order for that relationship to succeed. Yes, you will have to use forgiveness over and over again in your marriage. Forgiveness is a tool that must constantly be used in the handling of disagreements.

No matter how severe the wrong or disagreement is, you should always be willing to forgive. Don't let one disagreement destroy years of marital success. Let forgiveness be a tool that you are always willing to use when resolving disagreements with your spouse.

Every marriage will have disagreements, but those disagreements can be a tool that is used to make your marriage stronger and happier. Remember, the manner in which you deal with disagreements may highly affect the quality of your marriage. Every husband and wife should resolve right now to handle their disagreements in a proper manner.

Chapter 20

Keeping God in Your Marriage

The attack against marriage is no mistake. Satan has attacked the institution of marriage since its inception in the Garden of Eden. Marriage has been under attack through the entertainment industry, the sodomite movement and pornography. The influence of these three areas has done more to destroy marriage than anything else.

In order to keep your marriage strong enough to fight off these attacks, you are going to have to keep God in your marriage. Let me remind you that God is the One Who instituted marriage. If God started the institution of marriage, then I would think that God is the One Who can keep your marriage the strongest. Why would you leave out the One Who established the institution of marriage? That would be ridiculous!

No marriage is going to be what it ought to be unless God is a big part of it. Let me put this a different way. A wheel has a hub which it revolves around, likewise God is the hub that your marriage ought to revolve around. If you take God out of your marriage, then you will greatly struggle to have a happy marriage. Don't get me wrong, I do know there are people who have excluded God from their marriage and their marriage seems to be happy, but if God were included in their marriage, it would be an even better. There is no way a marriage can fulfill every feeling, love, emotion and closeness without God being involved.

If you are going to keep God in your marriage, then you are purposely going to have to include Him. Life tends to pull marriages away from God. Therefore, in order to keep your marriage strong, you and your spouse will have to purposely work together at making sure God is a daily part of your relationship.

The reason why it is so important to make God a part of your marriage is because no marriage can be truly happy without God. Psalm 1:1-3 says, *"Blessed is the man that walketh not in the counsel of the ungodly, nor standeth in the way of sinners, nor sitteth in the seat of the scornful. But his delight is in the law of the LORD; and in his law doth he meditate day and night. And he shall be like a tree planted by the rivers of water, that bringeth forth his fruit in his season; his leaf also shall not wither; and whatsoever he doeth shall prosper."* You could paraphrase the verses above by putting the word "marriage" where the word *"man"* is. In other words, you could put it this way, "Blessed is the marriage that..." The promises for the man in the verses above apply to your marriage as well.

The word *"blessed"* means "to be happy." In other words, in order for a person to be happy, God must be his delight. Likewise, for a marriage to be happy, God must be a part of that marriage. God promises His blessings upon the person or marriage that will make Him the hub around which they revolve.

Going further with this thought, God promises to add blessings to a person or institution that puts Him first. Matthew 6:33 says, *"But seek ye first the kingdom of God, and his righteousness; and all these things shall be added unto you."* Let's again include into this verse the thought of your marriage. We could put it this way, "But seek God first in your marriage..." This is not changing this verse for the truth of this verse applies to your marriage as well. God promises to bless the person or marriage that will seek Him first. If you will put God first in your marriage, then you will find God's blessings will rest upon your marriage.

As we have previously stated, in order to keep God in your marriage, you and your spouse will have to purposely work together as a team to be sure that He is the hub around which your marriage revolves. Let me give you several thoughts on how to keep God in your marriage.

1. Get saved!

There is no way that God can be a part of your marriage if you are not saved. Salvation is the foundation of your marriage revolving around God. If Jesus Christ is not your Saviour, then there is no way He can be the hub of your marriage. Though this may sound basic, it is important for you to make sure that you are saved.

Let me clarify that the only way a person can get saved is through accepting Jesus Christ and His payment upon the cross as the **only** payment for your sins. You cannot get saved through church membership, religious affiliation, baptism, good works or any other method. Your religious leader cannot save you, your background cannot save you and you have not always been saved. Everyone is a sinner and must realize that their sins condemn them to Hell. Jesus Christ is the only One Who made the complete payment for sins. Jesus made that payment by dying on the cross and shedding His blood to be the atonement for your sins. After Jesus died, He was buried and spent three days and nights in the tomb after which He arose from the dead. Now Jesus is in Heaven and offers salvation to anyone who will accept it. If you are going to be saved, then you must accept the whole payment that Jesus made and put your complete trust in Him and Him alone to be your Saviour from your sins. Once you accept Jesus as your Saviour, you are then saved forever!

You need to be 100% sure that you are saved. You don't have to wonder if you are saved. You can know that you are saved if you will simply trust Jesus Christ as your Saviour. Wondering and hoping that you're saved is not good enough; you need to settle it once and for all by praying and asking Jesus Christ to save you from your sins. The Scriptures say in Romans 10:13, *"For whosoever shall call upon the name of the Lord shall be saved."* God promises that if you will call upon Jesus Christ to be your Saviour that He will save you from your sins and Hell, and your destination will then become Heaven when you die. Without this being accomplished, you will never be able to include God in your marriage the way that you should.

If you truly love your spouse, then you need to settle your salvation. For your spouse to be saved and you to continue being unsaved is not showing much love at all. How can you say that you love your spouse and not give them the hope to see you again if you were to die? If you truly love your spouse, you will accept Christ as your Saviour. When both you and your spouse are saved, then you both have the hope of seeing each other in Heaven when you die. Furthermore, with both you and your spouse being saved you have now taken the first step in making God the hub of your marriage.

2. Have a good church.

It is very important that you find a good church that you can regularly attend. There is no way that God is going to be an important part of your marriage if you don't attend a good church on a regular basis. God says in Hebrews 10:25, *"Not forsaking the assembling of ourselves together, as the manner of some is; but exhorting one another: and so much the more, as ye see the day approaching."* Just as it is important as an individual to regularly attend church, likewise it is important for a married couple to regularly attend church together.

When I say a good church, I believe there are several things which you should look for in a church. I believe you ought to make an independent Baptist church the church that you join. There are several reasons for this that I cannot get into in this chapter, but that is the first area in which you should look for a church. Then your church should stand firmly on the King James Bible. If you don't have the right Bible, then you cannot have a firm foundation to stand upon in your marriage. Your church should be separated from the world. You should not attend a church that looks and acts like the world. You should attend a church that is separated and not afraid to take a stand for Christ. Your church should be an aggressive, soul-winning church. Soul winning means that your church is not only concerned with the souls of men, but it shows that concern by regularly approaching people with their need of salvation. If you go to a church that does not aggressively go after the souls of men, then you ought to reconsider your home church. Your church should also have a pastor who preaches the whole counsel of God. In other words, your preacher should be balanced in his preaching and should also preach everything that the Scriptures tell him to. These are just a few guidelines of what you should look for in a church. Be sure for the sake of your marriage that you have a good church that you regularly attend.

3. Be faithful to church activities.

Just as it is important to have a good church, it is also important to be faithful to the activities of that church. What is the purpose of having a good church if you are not faithful to the activities of that church? You should make sure that you attend every service of your church. Don't just attend one or two services a week, but be sure to attend every service that your church has.

Likewise, be involved in the extra activities of the church. For instance, if your church has a church picnic, attend that picnic. If your church plans activities during the holiday season, then make sure that you and your spouse are present at those activities. Your marriage will be stronger when the church and not the world put on the activities that you and your spouse attend together. You need to make your church an intricate part of your marriage and one way you can do this is by attending church activities together.

4. Join a church ministry together.

I believe it is very important that you and your spouse work as a team in a ministry of your church. Though there may be ministries that you and your spouse work in individually, I believe it is best that the main ministry that you and your spouse work in is one that you do together. It will help your marriage to work as a team. If you're not careful, you and your spouse will get wrapped up in so many different ministries apart from each other that you are never in the church together. This is not good! Husband and wife are a team, and when you work in separate ministries, then it is hard to keep the same agenda in your marriage.

One of the reasons it is important to be in the same ministry is so that you and your spouse can go soul winning together. One of the greatest boosts to your marriage will be winning souls to Christ together. When you can go home and rejoice together over the victory of winning souls, then that will help to tighten the bonds of your marriage.

One caution I want to give you is to be careful about getting so involved in the ministries of the church that you are never home. Though this is a rare occasion, there are some who are so heavily involved in the church that their marriage sometimes suffers. I believe there is a good balance for your marriage in the amount of involvement you have in church ministries. I say this guardedly because I know there will be some lazy Christians who will use this as their excuse for not getting involved. Let me put it this way, if you are not involved in at least two ministries of your church, then this point is not for you. This is only to caution some from getting so involved that they never have time together.

5. Plan your schedule around the church schedule.

It is important to remember that God is the hub around which your marriage should revolve. In order to make God the hub of your marriage, then you need to be sure to plan all of your family activities around the church's schedule. As soon as I say this, I know there are some who will immediately cringe at this statement. The fact is, if we are going to seek God first as Matthew 6:33 commands us to, then we are going to have to plan every activity of our life around the church calendar.

Most churches have their year of activities and special services planned a year in advance. With this in mind, you should plan your vacations and personal activities around that schedule. Don't plan a vacation the week your church is going to have a conference or revival meeting. The conference or revival meeting ought to be a part of the schedule for your marriage. These are as important to keeping your marriage strong as being sweet with each other and spending time alone. If you are going to keep God in your marriage, then you need to be sure to plan your yearly schedule of events around the church's schedule. It should not be that the church has to plan around your schedule; it should be that you plan your schedule around the church's schedule.

6. Daily have a personal walk with God.

You will never be the spouse that you are supposed to be unless you daily spend personal time with God in the Scriptures and prayer. If you don't walk with God, then He will not be a part of your marriage.

Having a personal walk with God on a daily basis will make you a better spouse. Having a personal walk with God on a daily basis will certainly make you a better Christian. If you are a better Christian, then there is no doubt that you will be a better spouse. To think that a personal walk with God is not that important is like taking the hub out of the wheel; it just won't work. When you don't include God as a part of your daily life, then you are taking God out of the hub of your life and replacing Him with yourself. We are never to be the hub of our own lives; only God is to hold that position. When you place God first, then He can bless every other part of your life.

My wife knows that every morning I spend time with God studying the Scriptures and praying. During this time, she knows to leave me alone. Likewise, my wife also has a personal time with God every morning. During this time, I make sure that I leave her alone. In order for you to have a personal walk with God on a daily basis, you need to set that time in stone and make it a part of your daily schedule that you do not miss. Remember, having a personal walk with God will make you a better spouse. On the other hand, not having a personal walk with God on a daily basis will hinder your ability to be a good spouse. I don't think you want the latter, so be sure to spend some time daily studying the Scriptures and praying.

7. Pray together

One way to keep God as the hub of your marriage is to daily pray together as a husband and wife. This time of praying together is apart from your personal time with God. It would be good to start your day out together by praying. Before you leave the house to go to work, it would be wise to pray together for God's blessings and protection on your marriage while you are apart from each other. Likewise, it would be good to end your day praying together. Before you go to bed at night, spend a short time praying together. Never leave each other's presence without praying together. Let God become so important in your marriage that you talk to Him before you leave each other's presence.

When you start having prayers answered that you and your spouse prayed for together, it will give a sense of victory to your marriage. There is nothing like having your prayers answered when you both have committed together to see God answer them. Praying together is another tie that will bind your marriage. The more ties that you experience together, the more secure your marriage will become.

8. Don't accept employment that takes you out of church.

Let me remind you what Matthew 6:33 says, *"But seek ye first the kingdom of God, and his righteousness; and all these things shall be added unto you."* In an effort to pay the bills, you must be careful not to accept employment that will take you out of church. God promises to take care of you if you will seek Him first. I know in today's world we think that we have to take what we can in order to pay the bills, but God is very capable of giving you the job you need if you will keep Him first and not accept employment that takes you out of church.

Having a job is important, but having God as a part of your marriage is more important. I have watched couples accept employment that takes them out of church, and then watch their marriage relationship drift apart. If you want to keep God in your marriage, then be careful about where you work. Be sure to take a job that will allow you to regularly attend all the church services.

9. Talk to each other about spiritual things.

One of the areas that many marriages lack in is in conversations about spiritual matters. Let me make this clear, if God is the hub of your marriage, then you will talk about spiritual matters. If God is the hub around which your marriage revolves, then there is no doubt that you and your spouse will have many conversations concerning spiritual matters.

Make some of your daily conversations about something you learned from your personal time with God. It is

211

not uncommon for my wife and I to discuss things we saw or learned from our time with God in the morning. Likewise, you can talk about God's blessings on your church. It is good to talk about God working in your church, for if God is a part of your marriage, then the church will also be an important part of your marriage. Having conversations that are spiritual are important if you want to have a spiritual marriage. If God is going to be a part of your marriage, then your conversations are going to have to be about subjects to which God would want to listen.

Keeping God in your marriage will take work. For your marriage to be what God intended for it to be, then you and your spouse will have to purposely keep God as the hub around which your marriage revolves. When God is the hub of your marriage, then you will have a happy marriage. The easiest way to make sure that your marriage is successful is to keep God as the hub. This is a fail proof piece of advice for every marriage. It won't be easy, but having God as the hub of your marriage will result in you and your spouse having the proper love and priorities toward each other and God.

Chapter 21

Keeping Yourself

You promised your spouse when you got married that "...for better or for worse..." you would stay married to them. Unfortunately some got "worse" after they got married. When I say the "worse" part, I am not talking about their spouse having a crippling or deadly disease, though that part of your vows certainly includes this. What I am talking about is having a spouse who turned out to be someone whom you did not expect them to be.

One of the goals in your marriage should be to make sure that you get better and not worse for your spouse. You want your spouse to feel that when they married you they got the "better" side of those vows. Of course, this can happen through your attitude and treatment of your spouse. You should want your spouse to think that one of the best decisions they made in their life was to marry you.

Another way you can help your spouse get the "better" side of the marriage vows is to work on keeping yourself in good physical shape. Just because you are married does not give you an excuse to let your appearance go. You should constantly work on your appearance so that your spouse can be proud to say they are married to you. You should constantly work on keeping yourself in good shape for this was part of the vows that you made to your spouse when you got married.

In the Song of Solomon, we find that the couple in this marriage worked on keeping themselves physically fit and looking sharp for each other. Notice what the husband says about his wife in Song of Solomon 4:1-3, *"Behold, thou art fair, my love; behold, thou art fair; thou hast doves' eyes within thy locks: thy hair is as a flock of goats, that appear from mount Gilead. Thy teeth are like a flock of sheep that are even shorn, which came up from the washing; whereof every one bear twins, and none is barren among them. Thy lips are like a thread of scarlet, and thy speech is comely: thy temples are like a piece of a pomegranate within thy locks."* You will notice that the husband is talking about the appearance of his wife. He is bragging on her appearance and how beautiful she was to him. He finishes talking about her in verse 7 when he says, *"Thou art all fair, my love; there is no spot in thee."* He looked at his wife and said he could not find one spot in her. In other words, she worked so hard at looking good for her husband that he was ravished with her appearance. This wife succeeded in keeping herself in good physical shape as well as having a sharp physical appearance in how she dressed. This caused her husband to have eyes for her and her alone.

The next chapter you see the wife bragging about how her husband kept himself looking sharp for her. The wife says about her husband in Song of Solomon 5:10-16, *"My beloved is white and ruddy, the chiefest among ten thousand. His head is as the most fine gold, his locks are bushy, and black as a raven. His eyes are as the eyes of doves by the rivers of waters, washed with milk, and fitly set. His cheeks are as a bed of spices, as sweet flowers: his lips like lilies, dropping sweet smelling myrrh. His hands are as gold rings set with the beryl: his belly is as bright ivory overlaid with sapphires. His legs are as pillars of marble, set upon sockets of fine gold: his countenance is as Lebanon, excellent as the cedars. His mouth is most sweet: yea, he is altogether lovely. This is my beloved, and this is my friend, O daughters of Jerusalem."* In this marriage, not only did the wife work at dressing sharp and keeping herself in good physical shape for her husband, but the husband worked on his appearance and physical conditioning as well. Keeping themselves in shape for each other was very important to this couple.

One way you can add spice to your marriage and keep your spouse looking only at you is to work on your physical conditioning and appearance. You should look and dress in such a way that your spouse is proud to identify with you. Too many couples let themselves get out of shape physically once they get married. Then once they are physically out of shape they begin to let their appearance become sloppy to the point where they just don't care about how they look. You should care how you look for one person, your spouse. The purpose of dressing sharp and staying in good physical condition is not to impress the men or ladies on the job. The purpose is to show your spouse you love them enough to work hard at keeping yourself for them.

I am not going to lie to you; it will take work if you are going to keep yourself for your spouse. The older you get, the harder it will be to keep yourself. Though you should not be worried about looking like Hollywood stars, you should work at looking as sharp as you can for your spouse. Let me give you some areas that you should work on in keeping yourself for your spouse. Some of these areas may seem very basic, but I will mention them for the sake of some who need to be reminded of them every once in awhile.

1. Dress sharp

Your appearance can be vastly improved by how you dress. When you get married you should be careful to not let your dress become sloppy. Far too many couples start dressing down after they get married when what they should be doing is dressing up for their spouse.

For instance, don't be sloppily dressed around the house. Just because you are home does not mean that you should look like a slob. Listen, get up and get dressed for the day instead of walking around in your sleeping apparel.

Though you are at home, your spouse should feel special enough that you would get dressed for them. How sad that when someone comes over to the house you dress up for them, but you never get up and get dressed for your spouse. Get out of your sleeping apparel and get dressed for the day so that your spouse feels that they are special. A good rule of thumb in this area would be to make sure that you are dressed for the day no later than eight o'clock in the morning.

Likewise, you shouldn't run around in old worn-out clothing all day. If you are going to do some work that requires that type of clothing then that is fine, but you shouldn't walk around in blue jeans with holes in them. Get some sharp casual clothing to wear around the house for your spouse. Look good for them and they will probably start dressing up for you. Even if they don't dress sharp for you, you need to be sure that you look sharp for them.

Be sure to iron your clothes and learn to dress in such a manner that you wouldn't be embarrassed if someone came over unexpectedly. You don't have to have expensive clothing to look sharp. You can look sharp by taking care of the clothing you have. Matching your colors accordingly and ironing your clothes can help you in dressing sharp.

2. Stay clean

I am embarrassed to have to bring this up, but when you travel as much as I do, you realize how dirty people are. Taking a daily shower is not that difficult. My mom used to say, "Cleanliness is next to godliness." Though the Scriptures don't say this, I believe my mom was right. If you are not concerned with your outward appearance, then I would imagine you are not that concerned with the cleanliness of your inner life either.

Staying clean is not just a good thing for you to do for your spouse, but it is physically good for you as well. Taking a daily shower can wash off germs that might cause you to get sick. Though staying clean seems to be something that is obvious, be sure that you are not guilty of rarely cleaning up. Simply stated, take a shower every day!

3. Smell good

Song of Solomon 3:6 says, *"Who is this that cometh out of the wilderness like pillars of smoke, perfumed with myrrh and frankincense, with all powders of the merchant?"* When you read the whole chapter, you will notice that this is the wife talking about her husband. This is not the wife who smells good, but this is the husband who smells good for his wife.

You should work at smelling good for your spouse. First of all, deodorant is a wonderful thing that will help you to smell good. Again, you may think it is ridiculous for me to bring this up, but when you constantly sit next to people in airports and or airplanes whom you want to give a stick of deodorant because of their smell, then you would understand why I bring this up. There is nothing wrong with using deodorant, and I am sure your spouse would appreciate it as well.

Moreover, using cologne or perfume to smell good for your spouse is certainly something you should consider. Find out the cologne or perfume your spouse likes on you and wear it for them. If God thought it was important enough to put a verse in the Scriptures to show the good smell the husband had for his wife, then I would think that you should take this lesson and apply it to yourself, and try to smell good for your spouse at all times.

4. Stay in good physical condition.

Before I embark upon this topic, let me make two statements to you. First of all, be careful about comparing yourself to others. Don't fall for the trap of comparing your body to those portrayed in Hollywood. You are not trying to stay in good physical condition to show your body off to lustful eyes. You are staying in good physical condition for your spouse. Likewise, don't compare your spouse to others. If you are comparing your spouse to others, then that would mean that you are looking at others and this is wrong. Secondly, remember that everybody's body is different. Some will struggle in this area more than others.

With that said, let me challenge you to work at staying at a healthy weight. Though some will struggle at this more than others, and though age will play a part in this as well, you should constantly work at staying at a healthy weight. The danger for some is once they start gaining weight, if they are not careful, they will get to the point where they just don't care and that is when they start adding a lot of weight. Being overweight is not only wrong, but it is unhealthy as well. You might not be able to get back down to the weight you were when you were married, but you can work at keeping your weight down.

One way to keep your weight down is to eat a proper diet. Just to let you know, I am not a health food nut. I believe in eating a balanced diet. You could help keep your weight down by cutting back on the portions that you eat. You could also keep your weight down by cutting back on the sweets. Just these two areas alone will help a lot in controlling your weight. By the way, the sodas you drink are filled with sugar, cutting back on them will also help.

Furthermore, having a regular exercise regimen will help you to control your weight. Proverbs 31:17 says, *"She girdeth her loins with strength, and strengtheneth her arms."* This was talking about the virtuous woman. Notice that this lady worked on strengthening her arms. A virtuous woman is one who works on staying in good physical condition for her spouse. Likewise, in Song of Solomon 5:15, you will find that the husband worked on his physical conditioning.

I have found there are two ways to keep yourself in good physical condition. First of all, have a regular cardio workout. You can accomplish this by having a regular time to run or walk. You are not always going to feel like doing this, and sometimes you will have to kick yourself into gear and make yourself exercise. The second way is to have a strength-building time. I am not talking about being a body builder, but you can stay in good physical condition more easily by building your strength. I mention these things to help you to accomplish "keeping yourself" for your spouse.

5. Keep yourself properly groomed.

Grooming yourself for your spouse is part of keeping yourself for them. Ladies, painting your nails and having a good hairstyle will help you to feel good about your appearance and will also help your husband to feel proud of you. When it comes to hairstyle, I believe it would be wise for a wife to ask her husband what style he prefers. Of course, you must remember that the Scriptures say in 1 Corinthians 11:15 that a lady is to have long hair. So when it comes to looking for a hairstyle, look for one that includes long hair. By the way men, if your wife is going to groom herself in these ways, that means that you are going to have to give her some money to help her. Ladies, work at keeping yourself groomed for your husband.

Men, having a good haircut and being clean shaven is important. If your wife is going to work at keeping herself properly groomed, then you should work at grooming yourself as well. Keep your hair cut and combed. Again, 1 Corinthians 11:14 states that a man is to have short hair. So in keeping your hair groomed, be sure that you keep it cut short. Moreover, if your wife likes you to have a beard, then keep your beard trimmed and groomed. Your purpose for staying groomed is to keep yourself for your wife.

6. Stay healthy

I chose this one for last on purpose because too many times we let this area go until it is too late. Though I am not for running to the doctor for every sniffle that you get, I am for doing what you can to stay healthy. It is hard to love a spouse who is dead. Though death comes prematurely for some, we should do what we can to stay healthy for our spouse.

One way to stay healthy is to take a good multivitamin daily. Though I am not a doctor or health practitioner, I believe we can safely say that taking vitamins will help you stay healthy. Vitamins are a good preventative way to stay healthy.

Furthermore, when you start having health problems, go to your doctor and get yourself checked out. Your doctor cannot help you if you don't go to them. Likewise, your doctor can treat your problem more easily in the early stages than they can in the later stages of a disease or illness. It is wise to have regular check-ups to be sure that there is nothing going on in your body that you don't know about. There have been many times when a doctor has diagnosed something in someone who felt perfectly fine and they were able to treat it because they caught it at an early stage. Don't run from going to the doctor. God has given doctors wisdom to help us. When you're sick, go to the doctor so they can help you. Though a doctor visit is not enjoyable, for the sake of your spouse get your health taken care of quickly when you are dealing with sickness.

In closing, do your best to make your spouse feel that they got the "better" end of the "better or for worse" part of your vows. One way you can accomplish this is by keeping yourself in good physical condition and by dressing sharp. Implementing the ideas taught in this chapter will help you, and it is the least you could do for the one you love.

Chapter 22

A Work in Progress

As with anything that is worthy of your time and energy, your marriage will continue to be a work in progress until you go to Heaven. I don't mean to be negative, but your marriage is not always going to be in a state of a "happily ever after." Though this is your ultimate, you are going to hit some potholes and bumps on your marital journey. You must expect there to be some rough times, and you must allow those rough times to be building blocks for your marriage.

Every successful marriage is one that has been and will continue to be a work in progress. One of the things my grandfather stressed to me about their marriage was that they worked on their marriage and determined to happily grow old together. I believe that is one of the reasons why they have been married for over seventy years; they didn't give up when they hit the first bump. Instead, they continued working on making their marriage better. The result of this work is a marriage that is successful and happy.

Every person who reads this book needs to be realistic and understand that you are going to have problems in your marriage, but you and your spouse can take on the mentality that your marriage is a work in progress. As long as you will realize that your marriage is a work in progress, I believe you will find that your marriage will continually improve as the years progress. I am going to give you several ideas to help you as you work on your marriage.

1. Daily ask God to give you a happy marriage.

God says in Matthew 7:7, *"Ask, and it shall be given you; seek, and ye shall find; knock, and it shall be opened unto you:"* God promises us in this verse that if we will ask Him for something that He will give it to us. This is not just a passing thought by God. You can take this promise to the bank.

Daily I ask God to give me a happy marriage. As I make this statement you may be wondering if my wife and I are happily married. Let me assure you that we are! My reason for asking God to give me a happy marriage is because I know that He promises to give us that for which we ask. My wife and I desire to keep our marriage happy, so I ask God to give me a happy marriage so that He will continue to answer this request.

Your daily prayer concerning your marriage should be for God to give you a happy marriage. Claim the verse above as you pray this prayer. Don't wait for your marriage to be on the rocks before you start asking God to work in your marriage, but ask Him before you have marital problems so that you can avoid them. I prefer to pray in a preventative manner than a major overhaul manner. Asking God to give you a happy marriage is nothing more than praying in a preventative manner so that you may avoid marital problems. Ask God for a happy marriage while you continue to work on your marriage.

2. A marriage is always a work in progress.

Let me remind you that God is the One Who established marriage. Because God established the institution of marriage, then that means that your marriage is a work of God. God says in Philippians 1:6, *"Being confident of this very thing, that he which hath begun a good work in you will perform it until the day of Jesus Christ:"* God promises that He will continue to work on your marriage until He comes back.

Now if God is going to continue to work on your marriage, then most certainly you and your spouse should continue to work on it. You should never think that your marriage has arrived, but you should consistently realize that your marriage is a work in progress. The reason why it is a work in progress is because there are two sinners involved. As long as there are sinners involved in your marriage, then you will constantly have to work on your marriage until both you and your spouse are sinless. Being that you will not be sinless until you get to Heaven, your marriage will constantly have to be a work in progress if it is going to be successful. Don't ever stop working on your marriage. Constantly remember that it will be a work in progress until you go to Heaven.

3. Be patient with your spouse.

In 1 Corinthians 13, God shows us the attributes of charity. One of those attributes is that charity will be patient with its object. Notice what 1 Corinthians 13:4 says, *"Charity suffereth long, and is kind; charity envieth not; charity vaunteth not itself, is not puffed up,"* You will see that *"Charity suffereth long..."* In other words, charity will overlook many things in order to see the object of its work improve.

Because your marriage is a work in progress, you must be patient with your spouse. You spouse is not going to change over night into the spouse that God wants them to be. You must give them room to make mistakes, and you must give them time to grow into the spouse that they should be. Any work worth your effort is going to take patience. Your spouse is worth your patience, and you should patiently wait for them to become what they should be as a spouse.

When they make mistakes, don't blow up. When they make mistakes, be patient with them. When they make mistakes, give them the same space of grace to grow that you would want them to give you as you mature into a better spouse. Simply be patient with your spouse and don't be quick to jump on them when they make mistakes. You and your spouse are a work in progress; therefore you must be patient with each other as you work on improving yourselves.

4. Be patient with yourself.

God says in Galatians 6:9, *"And let us not be weary in well doing: for in due season we shall reap, if we faint not."* Notice that God warns us not to become *"...weary in well doing..."* Anything that is a work in progress can weary you to the point of giving up if you're not careful. God admonishes us to not get weary in doing good.

Many times I have seen people get so frustrated with themselves that they end up giving up. You cannot give up on yourself. You are going to make mistakes, and you cannot allow these mistakes to discourage you to quit trying. If you have not become the spouse you think you should be, be patient with yourself and understand that you are a work in progress, and that God is still working on making you into the spouse whom you should be. Don't get weary in becoming a better spouse. Be patient with yourself. Don't give up on yourself for your spouse's sake. Yes, you are going to make mistakes, but keep on working on those areas and be patient.

5. Don't get discouraged when your marriage isn't everything you think it should be.

Listen, I know that we all want our marriages to quickly progress into the image that we have for them. Yet, many times where your marriage is right now is not where you thought it would be. When that happens, you must not get discouraged with your marriage.

As Galatians 6:9 warns us, *"And let us not be weary in well doing: for in due season we shall reap, if we faint not."* If you don't give up on your marriage and continue to work on improving it, then you will reap good benefits for the work you have put into it. Let me remind you that between the planting of the seed and the reaping of the fruit, there will be many months of pulling weeds and pruning. If you will just hang in there, and don't let the discouragement of not being where you think you should be cause you to quit, then you will reap a great harvest of happiness in your marriage. Oh, your marriage may not be exactly where you think it should be, but don't let the discouragement of the slow progress cause you to give up.

6. Never stop working on improving your marriage.

Throughout this book, we have covered many topics concerning marriage. In every one of these areas, you must constantly work on them to improve your marriage. Your marriage will cease to improve if you stop working on it.

God intended for your marriage to get better as the years progress. When I married my wife, I thought that we had a great marriage from the very beginning. But I will be honest with you, what we had in the beginning years of our marriage is nothing compared to what we have right now. Our marriage has grown so much over the years and has improved far beyond what I could have ever imagined. The reason why is because neither my wife nor I have stopped working on our marriage. I look forward to where our marriage will be in twenty years if we both continue to work on it.

Likewise, your marriage will continue to improve if you and your spouse will continue to work on every area we have covered in this book. Continue working on your communication. Continue working on being more romantic with each other. Continue working on having a better relationship with your in-laws. On and on I could remind you

225

of the things you need to work on, but take the topics that have been covered and continue working on them. Never stop working on your marriage, for the day that you do is the day that your marriage will begin to die.

7. When you fail, get back up.

Proverbs 24:16 says, *"For a just man falleth seven times, and riseth up again: but the wicked shall fall into mischief."* In this verse, God is challenging us to become a person who gets back up after failure. God knew that we would fail in life, yet He challenges us to get back up and keep on trying to succeed at the work at which we failed.

When you fail in your marriage, you and your spouse need to decide to get back up and keep on working on improving your marriage. Though you may have failed over and over again, keep on getting up and work on that area of failure until you succeed. You both will have to make a conscious choice to continue to get up after failure. Remember, when you fail in your marriage, you are not the first one to fail. Be sure that you get back up and work at making it better.

8. Rejoice together over victories achieved.

When you and your spouse have a victory in your marriage, rejoice together over that victory. If we are not careful, we will focus so much on the failures that we forget to rejoice over the victories. By nature most people see the negative in life. Therefore, by nature you will see the failures in your marriage easier than you will see the victories.

Because of this, you and your spouse will have to purposely look for victories you have achieved in your marriage. When you see your spouse improve in an area, compliment them on their improvement. You don't have to preach at them and tell them you have been praying a long time for them in this area, but simply tell them that you appreciate their love for you by working on this area. Be quicker to rejoice over the victories in your marriage than you are to point out the failures. If you will make your marriage a work in progress, then you will experience many victories. When those victories occur, be sure to take some time to rejoice together over them.

9. Make personal goals that you want to achieve in your marriage.

I believe that most of the effort you spend on your marriage should be to improve yourself rather than trying to improve your spouse. I learned a long time ago that I could change myself a whole lot easier than I could change my wife. Because of this, I have put my efforts into improving myself as a husband instead of trying to change my wife.

With this is mind, you should set personal goals that you can work toward. You don't always have to let your spouse know in which areas you are trying to improve, but without a goal to strive towards in your marriage, you will never change your marriage. Goals have a way of motivating us to work harder. When setting goals for yourself, don't try to accomplish all of them at one time, but instead work on one goal at a time. You will become a better spouse much more quickly by having individual goals and working towards those goals.

10. Be flexible with your spouse.

If your marriage is going to improve, then you are going to have to be flexible with your spouse. Your marriage is a work in progress, and it will take flexibility on both sides for it to succeed. Things can't always be your way. Both you and your spouse must be flexible and be willing to work with each other as you work together on improving your marriage.

You must be careful not to adopt the mentality that it is either my way or the highway. If you adopt this mentality, then it won't be long before you are on the highway. Marriages that are successful are marriages where both spouses have learned to be flexible with each other. When you become flexible with your spouse, then your marriage will become workable. When your marriage becomes workable, then you will take great strides towards a happier marriage. Simply be flexible with your spouse so that you both can work together towards the desired goals in your marriage.

11. In your marriage, make a joint goal to happily grow old TOGETHER.

The ultimate goal of your marriage should be to happily grow old together. As we have previously discussed in this book, divorce is not an option. Therefore, your goal should be to grow old together. An even better goal is to happily grow old together. You should desire the benefits of experiencing a growing love for each other, as you grow old together.

Your marriage is supposed to be a work in progress so that it can improve over the years to the point where you could never imagine being without your spouse. Make your marriage a work in progress. Don't give up when the progress is slower than expected. If you will not become weary in the good work of improving your marriage, then when you get old you will reap the great benefits of those years of work. I truly believe that if you will realize that your marriage is a work in progress, then you will be more patient with each other as you press towards the ultimate goal of happily growing old together.

Chapter 23

Make It Work

Many topics have been covered in this book that I believe will help your marriage become better. Yet, I saved this chapter for last because if your marriage is going to make it, then both you and your spouse are going to have to decide that you are going to make it work one way or another.

In 1 Samuel 25, God described a marriage that was less than desirable. God says about the couple involved in this marriage, *"Now the name of the man was Nabal; and the name of his wife Abigail: and she was a woman of good understanding, and of a beautiful countenance: but the man was churlish and evil in his doings; and he was of the house of Caleb."* Abigail seemed to have married a person who was the complete opposite of her. When God described Abigail, He said she was a *"woman of good understanding, and of a beautiful countenance."* When God described her husband Nabal, He described him as *"churlish and evil."* The word *"churlish"* means, "to be rude." When you read the story of this marriage, you see that Abigail was the opposite of rude. She seemed to have good people skills. Somehow she ended up in a marriage relationship that wasn't the greatest. What I respect about this woman is that even though her husband wasn't easy to get along with, and her marriage didn't turn out the way she thought it would, she found a way to make her marriage work.

Sometimes people don't always turn out the way you thought they would. Many times in dating relationships, people will put on a facade to lure a good person to marry them, then after they are married, they revert back to their poor habits. When this happens to a person, they find themselves in a situation that they did not expect. If this happens to be your case, then you must find a way to make your marriage work.

Furthermore, there are times when a marriage just seems to struggle. For whatever reason, two good people struggle in their relationship with each other. Many times in this type of a relationship, the fault does not lie upon one spouse, but the fault lies upon both. In instances like this, the personalities or habits just don't seem to mesh. If this is your case, then you will just have to find a way to make your marriage work.

I will continue to say that divorce is not an option. Finding a way to work through your marital problems is the best way to solve those problems. Though you may have problems in your marriage, you and your spouse are going to have to determine to make your marriage work. If you did marry the wrong person, then once you got married you were married to the right person. Once you said, "I do," divorce is never an option. You made a promise to your spouse that for better or for worse you were going to stay married to them until death parts you. When problems arise in your marriage, you are just going to have to decide that you are going to make it work.

God says in Philippians 4:13, *"I can do all things through Christ which strengtheneth me."* God says in this verse that there is nothing you cannot work through if you will put your mind to it, and get God's help. No matter the obstacle that is hindering your marriage, you must decide to make it work one way or another. Let me give you a few thoughts on the above verse concerning your marriage.

1. *"I can"* is an attitude.

If you are going to make it work, then you are going to have to take on the attitude that you are going to make it work one way or another. If you believe there is no way that you can work through your problems, then you are right because if that is your attitude you can't. If that is your attitude, then your attitude is wrong. God says that anything is possible with His help and the right attitude.

You and your spouse must adopt the attitude that you are going to work through whatever problems may come your way. If you and your spouse will put your mind to making your marriage work out, then it will. It all starts with your attitude! You can't wait for your spouse to change their attitude; you have to be the first one to change your attitude, and decide to make it work. You have to decide that you can work through your problems. You may not know the way through the problems, but if you will have an "I can do it" attitude, then you are well on your way to finding the solution to making your marriage work in spite of your circumstances.

2. Making it work is not a choice.

Let me again make this very clear, **DIVORCE IS NOT AN OPTION!** When you decide to take divorce out of the vocabulary of your marriage, then making your marriage work will be the only other choice. You will never make your marriage work when you allow divorce to be an option. Both you and your spouse must firmly decide together that you will never allow divorce to be a consideration.

The only option that you and your spouse should ever consider concerning your marriage is to make it work. When this is the only choice you allow yourselves, then you have no other choice than to work out your problems.

3. Ask God to work in your hearts.

The way your marriage is going to heal from what ails it is to get God to work on the hearts of both you and your spouse. Just changing the heart of one spouse is not enough. In order to make your marriage work, you must ask God to change both hearts.

Whenever I have an issue with my wife, my prayer to God is to work on my heart first and then work on hers. I have found that God can do a better job of changing the situation than I can. If I try to change the situation, that only creates more friction and strife. So, if I can get God involved in changing our hearts, then I can solve every problem that my wife and I will ever have.

Ask God to change you in the areas that you need changing. Many times God will change us without us even realizing it. If God is working on your heart and you allow Him to change you, then you can make your marriage work. If both you and your spouse will ask God to work on your hearts in order to make your marriage work, then God can certainly do a work that you never could have imagined.

By the way, I am not just talking about asking God to change your hearts only when you have problems, I am also suggesting that you continually ask God to work on your hearts to improve your marriage at all times. Imagine if God was continually working on your hearts before you had marital problems. Imagine how much heartache you can avoid if God is working on your hearts at all times. Ask God to change whoever's heart needs to be changed and then be moldable enough to allow God to change you when He is working on you.

4. Decide that you are going to find a way to make your marriage work.

I close out this book by asking you to decide to find a way to make your marriage work. God intended for marriage to be enjoyable. To make your marriage happy and enjoyable, then you have to determine that you are not going to stop working on your marriage until you find the solution that makes your marriage work. Don't stop looking for the ways to make your marriage work. It is a decision you must make and this decision must be a firm decision.

In closing, let me tell you that my whole purpose for writing this book is to help you to have an enjoyable, happy marriage until death parts you. The words of this book were prayerfully written so that you and your spouse can happily grow old together. Though this is certainly not the only book on marriage, I do believe if you will follow the advice found in the pages of this book, you will live happily until death parts you.

I pray as you have read this book that the advice will be heartily taken so that you and your spouse will decide to make your marriage work; not just work, but find the true happiness that God intended for you to have. Marriage is a wonderful institution! Decide from this moment forward that you are going to make your marriage work. Decide that you won't stop working on your marriage until you have found true happiness in being married to your spouse. Decide to live happily with your spouse fulfilling the part of your marriage vows that said, "Till death do us part."